BOLTON WANDERERS MISCELLANY

WANDERERS HISTORY, TRIVIA, FACTS & STATS

BOLTON WANDERERS MISCELLANY

WANDERERS HISTORY, TRIVIA, FACTS & STATS

DEAN HAYES

BOLTON WANDERERS MISCELLANY

WANDERERS HISTORY, TRIVIA, FACTS & STATS

All statistics, facts and figures are correct as of 1st August 2008

Published By:
Pitch Publishing (Brighton) Ltd
A2 Yeoman Gate
Yeoman Way
Durrington
BN13 3QZ

Email: info@pitchpublishing.co.uk
Web: www.pitchpublishing.co.uk

First published 2008

10-digit ISBN: 1-9054112-1-9
13-digit ISBN: 978-1-9054112-1-4

Printed and bound in Great Britain by Cromwell Press

FOREWORD BY SIMON MARLAND

Having succeeded Des McBain as Bolton Wanderers' secretary, I can honestly say that I still experience the same excitement and pride working for the Whites today as I did many years ago when I joined the club as accountant. Nowadays, I deal with a number of tasks behind the scenes at The Reebok and like Dean, have also written a number of books on the club.

I've known Dean for a good number of years and I'm delighted to have been asked to write the foreword to this book. The book is not an exhaustive collection of statistics, nor is it an attempt to tell the history of the club from A to Z. The past and present of a football club is about much more than the sum of its results and its silverware. It is a rich tapestry comprised of personalities, traditions and defining moments, both on and off the pitch. The Bolton Wanderers Miscellany is a celebration of a unique club which has always been proud of its past and its traditions, while seeking to remain at the vanguard of progress and innovation.

Dipping in and out of this book, I've been reminded about a lot of things I already knew about the club and found out much more besides. If this publication succeeds in achieving its goal, then even the most seasoned and fanatical of Bolton supporters will, during a random excursion through the pages that follow, find something to surprise and intrigue them.

I'm certain that it won't be long before an updated version will be needed to record the landmarks the Wanderers are sure to set in the near future. Until then, I hope you enjoy reading the Bolton Wanderers Miscellany as much as I did.

Simon Marland
Bolton Wanderers Secretary

INTRODUCTION

As a small boy, I remember watching the 1958 FA Cup Final on my next door neighbours' television – as we didn't have one – and cheering on the Wanderers as they beat Manchester United 2-0. That day of course, the legendary Nat Lofthouse scored both Bolton goals and one of my favourite players, goalkeeper Eddie Hopkinson, kept a clean sheet. A year or so later, Lofty presented the prizes at my primary school and I was fortunate to shake hands with the great man as I won the 'Sportsman of the Year' award.

Whenever we played football in the school playground or the local park, I was always Eddie Hopkinson, but he wasn't between the posts as the Wanderers lost 4-1 at home to Newcastle United on my first-ever visit to Burnden Park in March 1960. I can still remember the day vividly as I rushed through the Great Lever End turnstiles to get my first view of the pitch and the stands that spread out before my eyes.

If I hadn't been hooked before, I certainly was then. Every Saturday was spent alternating between the different areas of the ground, watching the reserves when the first team were away until I somehow talked my mum and dad – although it was usually my mum – into travelling to away games.

Despite the depressing times of the late 1960s and early 1970s, which culminated in relegation to the third division for the first time, I remained a great optimist. By now I was standing on the Embankment End with friends and at half-time we would often re-enact the events of the first half by playing with a plastic cup, formerly filled with Bovril.

Eventually, I did get my wish to play on the hallowed turf in a Schools Cup Final. The tide eventually turned and having just started my teaching career at my former primary school, Brandwood, it became a joy to go to school on a Monday morning following a weekend of usually good results!

Life went full circle and in September 1986, I took my then three-year-old son Ben to his first game as Bolton beat Port Vale 3-0. Though, to be honest, I can't remember seeing any of the goals! That, though, was a disastrous campaign for the Whites as they dropped into the League's basement. After winning promotion at the first attempt, the Wanderers continued to have more than their share of ups and downs with the highlights including League Cup final appearances at Wembley and the Millennium Stadium, respectively, and of course, two journeys into Europe.

During my time as a primary school headteacher, I began to write sports books on a part-time basis and, having opted for a change to work as a sports journalist on a full-time basis, have recently had my 100th book published – three of which are on the Wanderers.

Despite now living in Pembrokeshire, I watch as many matches as is physically possible and for those I can't get to, I watch on television with a new, 86-year-old Bolton convert, Gerry Edenbrow, scorer at the cricket club I captain during the summer months.

My office houses one of my prized possessions – a photograph of myself with Big Sam at a press conference a few years back for a previous Bolton publication. I have thoroughly enjoyed compiling the Bolton Wanderers Miscellany and hope that it brings back some happy memories as well as offering some snippets of trivia to even the most learned of Bolton supporters.

Dean Hayes, 2008

IN THE BEGINNING

It was in 1874 when the club that was to become Bolton Wanderers FC was born. The Rev. JF Wright, the vicar of Christ Church was taking a great interest in the new sport of football, much of which was played in and around Bolton. He invited one of his regular churchgoers, schoolmaster Thomas Ogden, to collect sixpence from all interested players for the purpose of buying a ball. At that time, no standard set of rules had been agreed and matches were played against local teams with rules being made up almost as they went along. Meetings were held in Christ Church School but the vicar, who had been appointed president, refused to permit any business to be discussed unless he was present. Eventually, other members of the committee objected and, in August 1877, it was agreed to change the name of the club from Christ Church to Bolton Wanderers FC. Subsequent meetings were held at the Gladstone Hotel close to Pikes Lane, though the Wanderers moved headquarters again, this time to the Britannia Hotel at the corner of Deane Road, where they remained until becoming a limited company in 1895.

GATES CLOSED

The highest attendance for a game at Burnden Park came during the FA Cup fifth round match against Manchester City on 18 February 1933. The ground was bursting at the seams as 69,912 packed in to watch the game. Bolton had gone eight league games without a win so fielded an experimental side. City, who arrived only minutes before the kick-off due to traffic congestion, held the early initiative but Bolton took the lead through Jack Milsom. City then took the lead with two goals in the space of as many minutes from Eric Brook before Ray Westwood levelled the scores shortly before the hour mark. Alex Finney was then adjudged to have handled the ball on the line and Brook stepped up to convert the penalty and complete his hat-trick. A late goal from Fred Tilson gave City a 4-2 win. Burnden Park saw a less agreeable record four days later when a crowd of only 3,101 attended a first division match against Portsmouth – this being the smallest for a league fixture until November 1985.

BEST-EVER START

The Wanderers have been unbeaten for the first seven games of a season on three occasions: 1896/97, 1906/07 and 1934/35. Their best performance came in this latter season when they won all opening seven games, scoring 21 goals and conceding just two before losing 6-2 away to Sheffield United. However, that result didn't upset their rhythm because, the following week, Bolton thrashed Barnsley 8-0.

NORDIC WHITES

English managers like Scandinavian players because they are hard, tough and don't complain about the cold weather 'up north' in the winter. Here's a team of Whites from the fringes of the Arctic Circle.

Player	Nationality	Bolton debut season
Jussi Jaaskelainen	Finnish	1998/99
Stig Tofting	Danish	2001/02
Gudni Bergsson	Icelandic	1994/95
Per Frandsen	Danish	1996/97
Henrik Pedersen	Danish	2001/02
Claus Jensen	Danish	1998/99
Michael Johansen	Danish	1996/97
Mixu Paatelainen	Finnish	1994/95
Eider Gudjohnsen	Icelandic	1998/99
Bo Hansen	Danish	1998/99
Arnar Gunnlaugsson	Icelandic	1997/98

WORST START

There is nothing like a good start to a new season and Bolton's results at the opening of the 1902/03 season were nothing like a good start! It took 23 league games to record the first victory of the campaign, after drawing three and losing 19 matches. The run ended with a 3-1 success at Notts County on 17 January 1903 and the next four games were all won. Despite an improved run towards the end of the season, relegation to the second division could not be avoided.

HONOURS EVEN IN TEN-GOAL THRILLER

When Bolton entertained Chelsea at Burnden Park on 30 October 1937, Wanderers fans were hoping for something of an improvement, for in their last game, the Whites had gone down 4-1 at home to Preston North End. However, in drizzling rain and poor light, it was Chelsea who took an early lead through Wilf Chitty before Ray Westwood levelled for the Wanderers. Within a matter of minutes, Westwood had netted his and Bolton's second. Chelsea rallied and Jimmy Argue made the score 2-2 minutes before the interval. The second half began with two goals in as many minutes. Jack Calder restored the Wanderers' lead before Argue converted a cross by Chitty. Argue then put the Blues ahead and, in doing so, completed his hat-trick. Not to be outdone, Westwood scored his third and Bolton's fourth. It was still anybody's game and when Tom Grosvenor put Bolton in front with just five minutes remaining, it looked as though the Wanderers would win. But George Mills cleverly converted Argue's pass to earn Chelsea a point from this remarkable thriller.

JOE SMITH'S DOUBLE HAT-TRICK

One of the club's legendary forwards, Joe Smith, remains the only player in Bolton's history to have hit a double hat-trick. Joe's 'super six' though came in a wartime fixture as the Wanderers beat Stoke 9-2 on 23 September 1916. The following players have scored five goals in a match for Bolton.

Year	Player	Result
1882	Billy Struthers	Bolton 6 Bootle 1
1890	Jim Cassidy	Bolton 13 Sheffield United 0
1983	Tony Caldwell	Bolton 8 Walsall 1

JUST THE ONCE

There are four clubs that Bolton have met just once in home and away League fixtures during the course of a season. They are Loughborough Town (1899/1900), New Brighton (1899/1900), Colchester United (1987/88) and Scarborough (1887/88).

SPEEDO

At the start of the 2007/08 season, Welsh international Gary Speed was one of only three players who featured on the Premiership's bow in 1992. Having played for Leeds United and Everton, Speedo joined the Wanderers from Newcastle United for a fee of £750,000 in July 2004. He celebrated his 750th overall club appearance by scoring the first goal for Bolton against Liverpool on 30 September 2006. On 9 December 2006, Gary played in Bolton's 4-0 victory over West Ham United and, in doing so, became the first player in the history of the Premiership to make 500 appearances. On 25 August 2007, Speed scored with a powerful header for Bolton against Reading, making him the only player to have scored in every Premiership season. This feat was equalled by Ryan Giggs a couple of months later. A most popular player during his time at the Reebok, Speedo then left to join Sheffield United, initially on loan with a view to the deal becoming permanent.

NO PLACE LIKE HOME

The club has called several grounds home since it was founded in 1877.

Date	Ground
1877-1881	Dick Cockle's Field
1881-1895	Pikes Lane
1895-1997	Burnden Park
1997 to date	The Reebok Stadium

* prior to Dick Cockle's Field, the club, then known as Christ Church FC, played at the Park Recreation Ground.

MATCHSTICK PLAYMATES

In 1953 LS Lowry used the car park and the main stand at Burnden Park as the backdrop for his painting entitled 'The Match'. Burnden Park was also used the following year in the film Love Match, starring comedian Arthur Askey, in which a train driver pulls up on the ground's Embankment End to watch the game in progress.

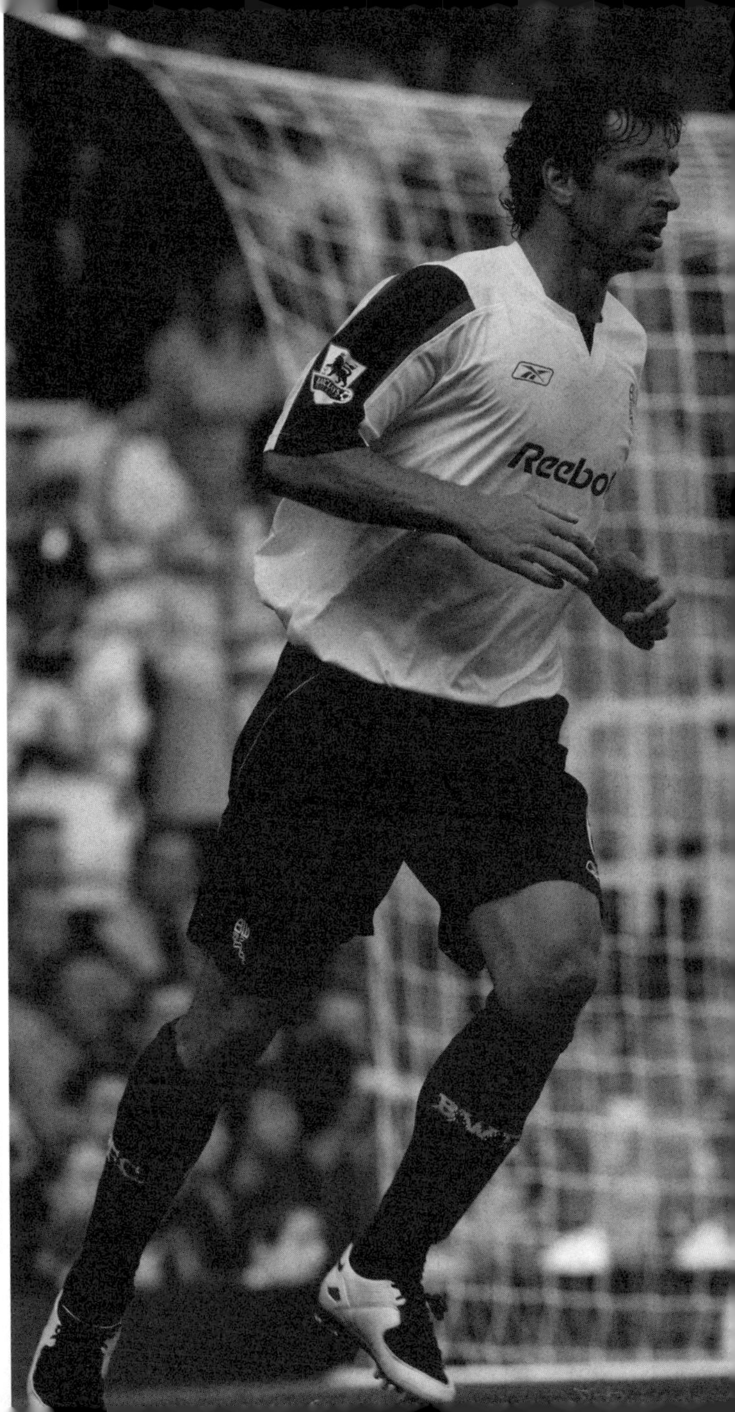

FIRST SUNDAY GAME

Bolton Wanderers made football history on 6 January 1974 by arranging the first major professional match on a Sunday. Within a few hours of hearing unofficially about the FA's decision to allow Sunday play in the third round of the FA Cup, Bolton had switched the game against Stoke City. They sought legal advice on the Sunday Observance Act and began to explore the most convenient way of admitting fans to Burnden Park whilst at the same time complying with law. Despite the heavy showers prior to the game, it didn't dampen those who would have the Sabbath kept holy with placards proclaiming 'Death is sure' and 'Christ is the answer'. No-one was allowed to buy a ticket but fans willingly paid 40p or 60p for a team-sheet that gained them admission. Whatever the arguments, soccer on a Sunday was a huge success with a crowd of 39,138 witnessing the proceedings – twice as big as Burnden's best that season! The game belonged to John Byrom and his hat-trick knocked out Stoke. The club's first league game on a Sunday came two weeks later when a Gil Merrick own goal and one from Roy Greaves gave the Whites a 2-1 win over Bristol City.

BAD DAY AT THE OFFICE

Bolton's record home defeats are:

0-6 v Chelsea ....8 Nov 1971, League Cup fourth-round replay
0-6 v Manchester United ....25 Feb 1996, in the Premiership

And away from home:

1-9 v Preston North End ...... 10 Dec 1887, FA Cup second-round tie

CHAMPIONSHIP SEASON I – 1908/09

Having suffered relegation the previous season, the Wanderers were looking to bounce back into the top flight at the first attempt. Early displays were mixed and after a run of three consecutive games without a goal in October, the Wanderers bought a number of players, including Jimmy Hogan and Billy Hughes. Both of them started to find the net on a regular basis and, at the turn of the year, Bolton were in second place. However, three games without any points at the start of the New Year saw them hanging on to third spot behind Tottenham and West Bromwich Albion, the Baggies also having knocked the Whites out of the FA Cup. It was now a three-horse race for the two promotion places and with four games left, just one point separated the three clubs. Albion beat Bolton 2-0 but then dropped a point in the next game, whilst both Bolton and Spurs won. Each of the leading three clubs had one game to play – strangely all had to play Derby County! Albion lost their final game against the Rams 2-1 whilst two days later, Spurs drew 1-1 at the Baseball Ground. This left the Wanderers to face County three days after the Spurs game in front of a 30,000 Burnden Park crowd. A goal from Billy Hughes, who scored 16 goals in 21 games gave Bolton a 1-0 win and the second division championship.

Football League Division Two

	P	W	D	L	F	A	Pts
BOLTON WANDERERS	38	24	4	10	59	28	52
Tottenham Hotspur	38	20	11	7	67	32	51
West Bromwich Albion	38	19	13	6	56	27	51
Hull City	38	19	6	13	63	39	44
Derby County	38	16	11	11	55	41	43
Oldham Athletic	38	17	6	15	55	43	40
Wolverhampton Wanderers	38	14	11	13	56	48	39
Glossop	38	15	8	15	57	53	38
Gainsborough Trinity	38	15	8	15	49	70	38
Fulham	38	13	11	14	58	48	37
Birmingham City	38	14	9	15	58	61	37
Leeds City	38	14	7	17	43	53	35
Grimsby Town	38	14	7	17	41	54	35
Burnley	38	13	7	18	51	58	33
Clapton Orient	38	12	9	17	37	49	33
Bradford Park Avenue	38	13	6	19	51	59	32
Barnsley	38	11	10	17	48	57	32
Stockport County	38	14	3	21	39	71	31
Chesterfield Town	38	11	8	19	37	67	30
Blackpool	38	9	11	18	46	68	29

INTERNATIONAL SCORING DEBUT

Five Wanderers players have scored on their full international debuts.

Player	Date	Match	Score
David Weir	2 Mar 1889	England v Ireland	6-1
Albert Shepherd	7 Apr 1906	England v Scotland	1-2
Nat Lofthouse*	22 Nov 1950	England v Yugoslavia	2-2
Ray Parry	18 Nov 1959	England v Northern Ireland	2-1
John McGinlay	20 Apr 1994	Scotland v Austria	2-1

Two goals

THE UNFRIENDLY FRIENDLY

When Bolton entertained Russian Army side CDSA under their new floodlights in November 1957, there were far too many unsavoury incidents. The Dutch referee was far too complacent, allowing the Russians to body-check and obstruct the Bolton players to their hearts' content. On the half-hour mark, Bolton centre-forward Nat Lofthouse was taken to the Royal Infirmary with concussion, this coming a couple of minutes after he had put the Wanderers 2-0 up following Ray Parry's opener moments earlier. Nat's replacement, Ralph Gubbins, added a third just before the interval but in the second half, the Russians, with six substitutions, did much better and reduced the arrears through Bukukin after 48 minutes. Joe Dean, in the Bolton goal, produced a number of top-class saves as the Wanderers held on to win 3-1 in a most bruising encounter. The longer the game wore on, the more tempers rose on both sides and consequently the football suffered.

BUSY TIME

In the season of 1993/94, Bolton played 64 competitive games – 46 in the league, eight in the FA Cup, four in the League Cup and six in the Anglo-Italian Tournament. Jason McAteer appeared in 62 of the games, missing the first two games of the Anglo-Italian Tournament against two of his future clubs, Tranmere Rovers and Sunderland.

WHAT'S IN A NICKNAME

Why are the Wanderers called the Trotters? The name has nothing whatsoever to do with the fondness of the Bolton people for the delicacy known by the name. Years ago, at the beginning of the 18th century, Bolton was famous for the number of practical jokers in the town. These gentlemen looked on strangers and visitors as their natural prey. The practice was known as 'trotting' and so widespread was the fame of some of these jokes that the reputation and the name struck to every Boltonian, who to the outside world became a 'trotter'.

INDIVIDUAL LEAGUE CUP SCORING FEATS

Player	Season	Opponent	Goals Scored
Nat Lofthouse	1960/61	Grimsby Town (h)	3
John Byrom	1969/70	Rochdale (h)	3
Garry Jones	1971/72	Manchester City (h)	3
John McGinlay	1996/97	Tottenham Hotspur (h)	3
Nathan Blake	1998/99	Hartlepool United (a)	3

WHAT A LOTTERY!

The Bolton Wanderers' Instant Lottery kicked off in December 1977, midway through the club's second division championship-winning season. The scheme was launched in the town's precinct by Bolton boss Ian Greaves and a number of his side's top players including Roy Greaves, Jim McDonagh and Neil Whatmore. A total of 90 newsagents were selling the £1000 draw tickets throughout the district. However, shortly afterwards, there was a cry of "offside" from neighbours Bury because they said the Wanderers had been selling tickets in their town!

A SHORT WORD FROM OUR SPONSORS

The first name ever to be featured on the famous white shirts of Bolton Wanderers was Knight Security. The other sponsors have been the Bolton Evening News, TSB, HB Electronics and Normid. The club's current sponsors are Reebok.

SPOT ON FRANNY

No one has scored more league goals from the penalty spot for Bolton Wanderers than Francis Lee. Having worked his way up through the ranks to make his debut as a 16-year-old amateur alongside Nat Lofthouse in November 1960, he scored one of the club's goals in a 3-1 win over Manchester City. He also got himself booked. One of the game's most deadliest of penalty takers, he first showed his prowess in a 5-4 defeat at West Bromwich Albion in September 1962 when he netted a hat-trick including scoring twice from the spot. Later, in his career with Manchester City, he was the first division's top scorer in 1971/72 with 35 goals, 15 of them penalties.

These are Bolton's leading penalty kings in league football.

Player	Penalties Scored
Francis Lee	26
Joe Smith	23
Tony Philliskirk	19
John McGinlay	16
Jeff Chandler	12
Steve Thompson	11
Ray Parry	10

LOST IN THE FOG

A rebuilt Manchester United, facing the Wanderers for the first time since the 1958 FA Cup Final meeting, arrived at Burnden Park to find the ground shrouded in fog. Although the game produced nine goals, much of the activity went unseen by large sections of the 33,358 crowd. It was a match laden with a cup-tie atmosphere – although conditions were only declared fit at 2.20 pm after experiments with the floodlights had only made matters worse. Apparently, goals were going in at both ends, one of which was a Ray Parry penalty for Bolton. The Wanderers were leading 5-3 in a game that was becoming farcical as no-one could see from one end of the pitch to the other. The scoring was completed by Ralph Gubbins, although no-one knew how the goal came about!

DING DONG DO

One of Wanderers best known supporters Dave 'Ding Dong Do' Higson, died on 1 March 2006. Dave was my cousin and provided the commentary on Bolton Wanderers videos for more than ten years when the club were based at Burnden Park. These commentaries made him a cult figure, earning him appearances on such TV shows as Oddballs and Fantasy Football. He was first asked to do commentaries for the videos in 1986 when his 'potential' was spotted while working in his spare time as a steward on one of the club's match coaches. He developed a good rapport with the players and management and knew that if he ribbed them in his reports, they would good naturedly get their own back. All true Bolton fans will have seen the videos and surely will have smiled at Dave's stock phrases: "Oh I do believe he's given a penalty", "Julian Darby, Jules as they call him here at Burnden Park", and, of course, the classic "Mark Winstanley! Goal! Mark Winstanley! Winnie, Winnie, Winnie!"

CONSECUTIVE HAT-TRICKS

Only one Bolton Wanderers player has scored hat-tricks for the club in two consecutive Football League matches. On 13 October 1928, Harold Blackmore scored three of the goals in Bolton's 4-2 home win over Portsmouth. A week later, in a game away to Aston Villa, he netted another treble in a 5-3 win for the Wanderers. The following game saw George Gibson get in on the act with a hat-trick in the 3-1 defeat of Sheffield United.

A 23-MATCH UNBEATEN RUN

On 6 October 1990, Bolton Wanderers lost 1-0 at home to Stoke City in what was their ninth league game of the season. Their record was then two wins, one draw and six defeats in the third division. But of their next 23 games, they won 15 and drew eight – the best run in the club's history. The sequence ended with a 4-0 defeat at Mansfield Town on 12 March 1991. The Wanderers reached the play-offs but after beating Bury over two legs, lost 1-0 to Tranmere Rovers in the play-off final at Wembley.

FA CUP FINAL 1894

In the sixth season of the Football League, Bolton Wanderers, for the first time, made it through to the FA Cup Final, which was played at Goodison Park. In opposition were second division Notts County but Bolton, who had finished thirteenth in the first division, were no match for their opponents. Sadly, it was matters off the field that overshadowed the Wanderers' appearance in the premier Cup competition. David Weir was not selected due to an individualistic temperament that caused arguments with other team members, whilst James Turner and David Willcocks were out injured. Four other players – Alex Paton, Harry Gardiner, Handel Bentley and John Somerville – were also carrying injuries but they all played. County took the lead after 20 minutes through Arthur Watson before Bolton's Archie Hughes became their fifth 'passenger' following a nasty tackle. County went 2-0 up just before half-time through James Logan and, though John Sutcliffe was performing heroics between the posts, he couldn't prevent Logan from adding two more early in the second half to complete his hat-trick. Wanderers' only consolation was a goal by James Cassidy late in the proceedings. Bolton's route to the final was as follows:

Round/Scorers	Opponents	Score
First	Small Heath (a)	4-3
Cassidy 2, Wilson 2		
Second	Newcastle United (a)	2-1
Hughes, Turner		
Third	Liverpool (h)	3-0
Cassidy, Dickenson 2		
Semi-final	Sheffield Wednesday(n)*	2-1
Bentley 2		
Final	Notts County (n)**	1-4
Cassidy		

*played at Fallowfield, Manchester
**played at Goodison Park, Liverpool

Bolton's 1894 FA Cup Final team was: Sutcliffe, Somerville, Jones, Paton, Hughes, Gardiner, Wilson, Tannahill, Cassidy, Dickenson, Bentley.

IT'S ALL BALLS

The first time that Bolton Wanderers supporters – or at least those with access to a wireless – were able to hear the FA Cup draw 'live' was when the BBC broadcast the third-round draw on 16 December 1935. On that occasion, the Trotters were handed a trip to Ewood Park, home of local first division rivals Blackburn Rovers. The game ended in a 1-1 draw, with Rovers winning the replay at Burnden Park 1-0. It is recorded that the FA Secretary Stanley Rous was requested that day "to ensure that the bag is shaken for a few seconds to produce a distinctive and suitable sound".

MOST CONSECUTIVE GAMES

Republic of Ireland international goalkeeper Jim McDonagh made 161 consecutive league appearances straight from his debut. The only other player to have played in more than 100 consecutive league games from his debut is former full-back and assistant-manager Phil Brown who played in 134 games. Here's the top ten longest run of league games by Bolton players:

Player	Dates	Games played
Jim McDonagh	2 Oct 1976 to 3 May 1980	161
Archie Freebairn	6 Oct 1894 to 21 Jan 1899	136
Phil Brown	27 Aug 1988 to 7 Apr 1991	134
Bryan Edwards	13 Nov 1954 to 26 Dec 1957	133
Barry Siddall	25 Aug 1973 to 25 Sep 1976	133
Warwick Rimmer	20 Mar 1964 to 22 Apr 1967	131
Mike Walsh	31 Dec 1977 to 6 Dec 1980	125
Peter Reid	21 Dec 1974 to 29 Oct 1977	125
Jussi Jaaskelainen	4 Jan 2005 to 2 Mar 2008	118
George T Taylor	23 Dec 1933 to 3 Oct 1936	117

FOOTBALLER OF THE YEAR

Only one Bolton Wanderers player has ever been honoured by the Football Writers' Association as their choice for Footballer of the Year – England centre-forward Nat Lofthouse in 1952/53.

CHOPPER HARTLE

Signed from Bromsgrove Rovers, full-back Roy Hartle made his Bolton debut in a 2-1 defeat at home to Charlton Athletic on New Year's Day 1953. Despite the reversal, Hartle had impressed and kept his place in the side for the next 24 games, which included seven matches in the club's run to the FA Cup Final at Wembley. However, he was devastated when he was dropped in favour of Johnny Ball for the showpiece against Stanley Matthews' Blackpool. After completing his National Service, the popular defender returned to win a regular place in the team and form, with Tommy Banks, the most feared full-back pairing in the Football League! Affectionately known as 'Chopper' – most opposition wingers would be able to tell you why – he was a virtual ever-present in the Wanderers' side for the next 11 seasons, often captaining the side. He won an FA Cup winners' medal in 1958 and was considered unlucky not to gain international recognition. He had played in 499 League and Cup games for the club when he left to end his playing career with non-league Buxton of the Cheshire League. Hartle, who served on the executive of the PFA, also spent a year coaching NASL side New York Generals before becoming chief scout at Bury.

POPULAR VISITORS

The following clubs achieved record attendances when Bolton Wanderers were the visitors.

Blackburn Rovers ....FA Cup sixth round, 2 Mar 1929 62,522
Bury ....FA Cup third round, 9 Jan 1960 35,000
Darlington ....Lge Cup third round, 14 Nov 1960 21,023

MAKING A SPECTACLE OF ONESELF

On St David's Day 1971, a crowd of just 943 saw the Wanderers defeat Ranger Freja – the first Danish side to play at Burnden Park – 2-1. The Danish side fielded a goalkeeper by the name of Bone, who wore spectacles. His task was made all the harder as the entire games was played in a snowstorm!

PLAY IT AGAIN SAM

Sam Allardyce, the towering figure at the heart of the Bolton defence in two spells with the club that saw him amass 231 League and Cup appearances, was the man that the Wanderers board turned to in their bid to lead the club back to the top flight. After losing in the play-offs in his first season in charge, Big Sam took the club back to the Premiership in 2000/01 when they defeated Preston North End 3-0 in the play-off final at the Millennium Stadium. Since then the Wanderers have remained in the top flight, reaching the League Cup final in 2004 and qualifying for Europe on two occasions prior to Sam's ill-fated departure to Newcastle United.

VIZARD THE WIZARD!

Winger Ted Vizard played rugby for Penarth and football for Barry Town before he was recommended to the Wanderers by an old school friend and invited to Burnden for a month's trial. The Wanderers signed him in September 1910 and he made his debut two months later in a 3-0 home win over Gainsborough Trinity. In January 1911, only two months after his Bolton debut, Vizard won the first of his 22 Welsh caps, his last coming in October 1926 when he was 37. During the First World War, Vizard served in the RAF and 'guested' for Chelsea alongside Joe Smith. The pair formed a great left-wing partnership and helped the Pensioners win the 1918 London v Lancashire Cup Final. In February 1919, the management of Bolton Wanderers was put in Vizard's hands until normal league football returned and Charles Foweraker was appointed. Ted Vizard was a member of Bolton's successful FA Cup-winning teams of 1923 and 1926 and though not a prolific scorer, he did score 13 goals in 1925/26 including all three in the 3-0 defeat of Arsenal. He made the last of his 512 League and Cup appearances – during which he scored 70 goals – on 21 March 1931. He was then 41, which makes him the oldest player to appear in a first team games for the Trotters. He then took charge of the 'A' team before leaving Burnden Park in April 1933 after almost 23 years' service. Vizard became manager of Swindon Town and later took charge of Queen's Park Rangers and Wolverhampton Wanderers.

BOLTON MANAGERS

Current incumbent Gary Megson is Bolton's 23rd manager. Whilst Sam Allardyce was one of the most popular, leading the club to the first division championship in 1996/97, the League Cup Final of 2004 and into Europe for the first time, spare a thought for ex-Burnley and Northern Ireland international Jimmy McIlroy, who was in charge of the club for just 18 days.

Manager	Years in Charge
Tom Rawsthorne (Secretary)	1874-1885
JJ Bentley (Secretary)	1885-1886
WG Struthers (Secretary)	1886-1887
Fitzroy Norris (Secretary)	1887
JJ Bentley (Secretary)	1887-1895
Harry Downs (Secretary)	1895-1896
Frank Brettell (Secretary)	1896-1898
John Somerville	1898-1910
Will Settle	1910-1915
Tom Mather	1915-1919
Charles Foweraker	1919-1944
Walter Rowley	1944-1950
Bill Ridding	1951-1968
Nat Lofthouse	1968-1970
Jimmy McIlroy	1970
Jimmy Meadows	1971
Nat Lofthouse	1971
(administrative manager to 1972)	
Jimmy Armfield	1971-1974
Ian Greaves	1974-1980
Stan Anderson	1980-1981
George Mulhall	1981-1982
John McGovern	1982-1985
Charlie Wright	1985
Phil Neal	1985-1992
Bruce Rioch	1992-1995
Roy McFarland	1995-1996
Colin Todd	1996-1999

Sam Allardyce 1999-2007
Sammy Lee 2007
Gary Megson 2007-

UNDERSOIL HEATING

At the end of the 1979-80 season, undersoil heating was installed at the Wanderers' former ground Burnden Park. The system was of Swedish design and operated by way of an oil-driven boiler feeding into an undersoil network of hot water pipes. The cost to the club to install the system was in the region of £70,000, which included 14 miles of heating pipes placed under the playing surface. At the same time major remedial work on levelling and draining the Burnden Park playing surface also took place.

MEET THE CHAIRMAN

The Bolton Wanderers FC chairman Phil Gartside is a local businessman. He was born during the Second World War, in August 1941 to be precise, in the town of Leigh, a few miles outside of Bolton. He grew up with a love of football from an early age, and as a young man he studied commerce at Trinity College, Dublin, throughout the early part of the Sixties. He had his first taste of Bolton Wanderers at the start of the following decade, when he saw Wanderers beat Aston Villa 1-0 at Burnden Park. He was immediately captivated by the passion of the Wanderers' fans and, when his then business partner James Connell offered him a season ticket, the Trotters quickly became a large part of his life. He was appointed on to the board of directors in 1988 and 11 years later he succeeded Gordon Hargreaves as the Bolton chairman. Having appointed Sam Allardyce as manager, he guided the club into a new era at the Reebok Stadium and promotion to the Premiership. Not only did the club consolidate their place in the Premiership under his chairmanship, but they have also been involved in two Uefa Cup campaigns. He has seen a number of high-profile footballers arrive at the club including Youri Djorkaeff, Jay-Jay Okocha and Nicolas Anelka. Phil Gartside is also a prominent football administrator and currently is a Football Association board member.

FA CUP FINAL 1904

Bolton's second appearance in the FA Cup Final found them as underdogs. After an indifferent season in the second division, in which they eventually finished seventh, they went up against a Manchester City team that had been chasing the first division title. City had the better of the early exchanges and thoroughly deserved their lead – scored by Welsh international Billy Meredith – even though he was a clear two yards offside. In the second half, the Wanderers produced some of the fine form that had defeated other top-flight clubs in the previous rounds but their finishing left a lot to be desired. Bolton were admired for their dogged perseverance but this did little to quell their great disappointment. Bolton's route to the final was as follows:

Round/Scorers	Opponents	Score
First	Reading (a)	1-1
Marsh		
First (replay)	Reading (h)	3-2
Freebairn, Marsh, Yenson		
Second	Southampton (h)	4-1
Marsh 2, White 2		
Third	Sheffield United (a)	2-0
Marsh, Yenson		
Semi-final	Derby County (n)*	1-0
Taylor		
Final	Manchester City (n)**	0-1

*played at Molineux, Wolverhampton
** played at Crystal Palace, London

Bolton's 1904 FA Cup Final team: Davies; Brown; Struthers; Clifford; Greenhalgh; Freebairn; Stokes; Marsh; Yenson; White; Taylor.

LOFTY THE LION

Football supporters don't come much bigger than Bolton Wanderers' nationwide favourite, Lofty the Lion. A bulky 6ft 6ins, he wears kit – extra, extra large – and his size 26 feet are encased in studded boots specially made by Reebok!

FOUNDER MEMBERS

Bolton Wanderers are one of the 12 founder members of the Football League, which held its inaugural season in 1888/89. The teams, which were either from the north-west or the Midlands, were: Accrington Stanley, Aston Villa, Blackburn Rovers, Bolton Wanderers, Burnley, Derby County, Everton, Notts County, Preston North End, Stoke, West Bromwich Albion and Wolverhampton Wanderers. Bolton entertained Derby County for their first-ever league fixture, but the Rams arrived late and the game began half-an-hour after the scheduled start. Bolton's first international player, Kenny Davenport, had the distinction of scoring the club's first-ever goal after only two minutes. He scored again a minute later and with James Brogan netting soon after, the Wanderers were 3-0 up after only five minutes! However, Derby came back to lead by half-time and ran out 6-3 winners. A week later, Burnley were the visitors to Pikes Lane and circumstances were again similar. Bolton led 3-0 but the Clarets came back to win 4-3. Another defeat followed the next week at the all-conquering Preston North End but then, on 29 September, the Wanderers chalked up their first league win, beating Everton 6-2. After a slow start, Bolton produced some impressive results and finished the inaugural season of league football in fifth place, 18 points behind runaway champions Preston.

MOST CLEAN SHEETS

Clean Sheet is the colloquial expression to describe a goalkeeper's performance when he does not conceded a goal. The highest number of clean sheets in a season kept by a Bolton keeper came in 1987/88 when the club won promotion from the fourth division at the first time of asking. Welsh international Dave Felgate kept 21 clean sheets in the 46-match league programme along with another couple in FA Cup and Sherpa Van Trophy games. The only other keeper to have kept more than 20 clean sheets in a league season is Dick Pym; 'The Topsham Fisherman' kept 20 in 1924/25 plus another in the FA Cup. Keith Branagan came close in the Wanderers' promotion-winning season of 1994/95 with 19 clean sheets in the league but he did keep a further four in Cup games.

TOTTENHAM PAY THE PENALTY

When it comes to scoring penalties, no club has had to endure more spot-kick woes against Bolton than Spurs. Wanderers have managed 16 penalties against them over the years, three more than they've scored against local rivals Preston North End.

Clubs	Penalties Scored
Tottenham Hotspur	16
Preston North End	13
Manchester City	10
West Bromwich Albion	10
Blackpool	9
Derby County	9
Huddersfield Town	9
Arsenal	8
Chelsea	8
Oldham Athletic	8

FRENCH FOREIGN LEGION

Aside from Englishmen, Bolton have relied on more French-born players during their first nine seasons in the Premiership than any other nation – no fewer than 12 in all.

Player	Date signed	From
Franck Passi	November 1999	Compostela
Mickael Kaprielian	January 2000	Martigues
Bruno N'Gotty	September 2001	Marseille
Youri Djorkaeff	February 2002	Kaiserslautern
Mario Espartero	February 2002	Metz
Bernard Mendy	July 2002	Paris St Germain
Pierre-Yves Andre	January 2003	Nantes
Florent Laville	February 2003	Lyon
Vincent Candela	January 2005	AS Roma
Fabrice Fernandes	August 2005	Southampton
Nicolas Anelka	August 2006	Fenerbahçe
Gerald Cid	July 2007	Istres

HAPPY HUNTING GROUND

Deepdale was certainly a happy hunting ground for Bolton Wanderers in a six-year spell between 1963 and 1969. During that period, Preston North End lost four and drew two of their games with Bolton on their own territory. Bolton scored 14 goals in the six league games, including four in a 4-1 win in November 1968 and a Francis Lee hat-trick in a 3-1 triumph in February 1967. The Wanderers also won 2-1 at Deepdale during this period in an FA Cup fourth-round tie in 1964/65, though they did go down 3-2 in the same competition the following season.

CROWD TROUBLE

However unwelcome, crowd disturbances are far from a modern phenomena at major football matches and there was plenty of hooliganism and disorder at matches in the 19th century. The first occasion in which the Bolton crowd was involved in misbehaviour was back in the pre-League days of 1883 when referee Sam Ormerod was booed from the field at Pikes Lane and then assaulted at the town's railway station. It was recommended that the Wanderers be expelled from the Lancashire FA for failing to protect him, but the Football Association decided not to take any action. The Pikes Lane ground became a very uncomfortable place for visitors and referees alike, who were greeted with 'hooting' and criticism.

ONE IN THE EYE

After nearly ten weeks' lay off through unfit grounds during the 1962/63 season, Bolton returned to action with a game against Arsenal at Highbury. Though the Gunners led 1-0 at half-time, goals from Freddie Hill and Dennis Butler gave Bolton the lead before the home side levelled. With only seconds remaining, Bryan Edwards gave away a free-kick which Armstrong swung into the penalty area. Normally Eddie Hopkinson would have swallowed it but under a challenge from Geoff Strong, who accidentally poked the Bolton keeper in the eye, he allowed the ball to sail straight into the net. The England international later took full blame for his team-mates' lost bonus.

THE BIG FREEZE

The freezing conditions of the winter of 1963 forced many postponements in England. Between 8 December 1962 and 9 March 1963, Bolton were to play only one league game – a 3-2 defeat at Arsenal, where Highbury had undersoil heating. So club officials organised for the Wanderers to travel to Ireland to get some match practice. Their opponents in Cork were Manchester United, who won the friendly 4-2. The third-round FA Cup tie against Sheffield United at Bramall Lane was played at the thirteenth attempt but there was little joy for the Wanderers, who went down 3-1. There was immediate revenge, however, for the Blades then visited Burnden Park in the club's first home game for three months. A Freddie Hill hat-trick secured the points as the Wanderers fielded their youngest-ever forward line.

NEW YEAR'S DAY EXTRAVAGANZA

On New Year's Day 1930, Bolton hammered Huddersfield Town 7-1. The Wanderers had beaten the Yorkshire side 2-0 some 11 days earlier at Leeds Road, since when both teams had won three games. Billy Butler netted a hat-trick and then the next three Bolton goals, scored by Willy Cook and Harold Blackmore (2), came in the space of just four minutes before George Gibson rounded off the scoring for the Wanderers.

MANAGER FOR 18 DAYS!

Former Burnley, Stoke and Northern Ireland inside-forward Jimmy McIlroy, who won 55 caps for his country, was appointed manager of Bolton on 4 November 1970. His first game in charge was a 1-0 home defeat at the hands of Norwich City, followed by a 2-0 reversal at Millwall a week later. A Roger Hunt hat-trick helped the Wanderers beat Birmingham City 3-0 but the following day, McIlroy parted company with the club. No official reason was given but offers had been invited for a number of key players. If they had left, it would no doubt have further weakened the team and it was obvious that the Irishman could not work within those constraints.

ABANDONED MATCHES

On Boxing Day 1882, with Nottingham Forest leading the Wanderers 3-1, the referee made some indifferent decisions, which resulted in the Forest players leaving the field and refusing to return! On Christmas Day 1885, Bolton were leading Great Lever 2-1 at Woodside. The crowd began fighting and this spread to the players, leaving the officials no option but to abandon the game. Wanderers' star James Turner was the centre of a furore which saw the abandonment of a Lancashire Cup tie at Bury in March 1893, when the crowd rushed on the field of play to attack him after he was involved in a fracas with an opponent. On Christmas Day 1937, Bolton's game against Derby County was abandoned due to fog before the first half was over with the Wanderers leading 2-0. The Bolton players were of the opinion that the fog was certainly no worse at that time than it was at the beginning of the game. On New Year's Day 1979, Peter Reid broke his leg in a collision with Everton goalkeeper George Wood on a snow-covered Burnden Park pitch, the game later being abandoned. The last game involving the Wanderers at Burnden Park to be abandoned was in 1989 when a waterlogged pitch ended the game with Wigan Athletic.

INTO THE CUP

Bolton first participated in the FA Cup in October 1881 when two own goals helped them draw 5-5 at home to Eagley. In the replay, the only goal of the game was scored by Bolton's Billy Steel to set up a second-round tie at Blackburn Rovers. Despite James Atherton and Billy Struthers scoring for the Wanderers as they had done in the first-ever Cup game against Eagley, it was Rovers who ran out winners 6-2.

FA CUP FINAL 1923

Known as the 'White Horse' final, this was Wembley's first final and it nearly became a disaster. Though 126,047 people paid for admission, thousands more burst down the doors to invade the stadium. It is believed that almost 200,000 were present at kick-off time, when the pitch was completely covered by spectators. As the Bolton players stood on the edge of the pitch watching the police horse clear the playing area, someone tapped John (JR) Smith on the back. It was his brother, whom he hadn't seen for over six years! It was largely due to the patience of the famous policeman on his white horse that the pitch was cleared, but even so, spectators still encroached on to the pitch during play. However, it was felt safer to play the game than to announce to the hordes that the match would be postponed. Within two minutes of the eventual kick-off, which was delayed by 40 minutes, David Jack had scored for the Wanderers. Both teams remained on the pitch at half-time and eight minutes after the break, Bolton scored again. Taking a pass from Ted Vizard, JR Smith rammed the ball home with his left foot with such force that it hit the crowd wedged in behind the goal and rebounded onto the pitch. Many people didn't know a goal had been scored until West Ham kicked off again. Thus, in such bizarre circumstances, did Bolton secure the FA Cup for the first time in their history. Bolton's route to the final was as follows:

Round/scorers	Opposition	Score
First	Norwich City (a)	2-0
J Smith, JR Smith		
Second	Leeds United (h)	3-1
Jack 2, J Smith		
Third	Huddersfield Town (a)	1-1
Jack		
Third (replay)	Huddersfield Town (h)	1-0
Jack		
Fourth	Charlton Athletic (a)	1-0
Jack		
Semi-final	Sheffield United (n)*	1-0
Jack		
Final	West Ham United (n)**	2-0
Jack, JR Smith		

*played at Old Trafford, Manchester
** played at Wembley Stadium

Bolton's 1923 FA Cup Final team was: Pym, Haworth, Finney, Nuttall, Seddon, Jennings, Butler, Jack, JR Smith, J Smith, Vizard.

THE ICELANDER COMETH

Gudni Bergsson was a law student at Reykjavik University when he was invited to join Spurs on trial. He was playing as an amateur for his local club, whom he helped win the Icelandic title in 1987 and the Icelandic Cup in 1988. With Spurs he appeared in 87 League and Cup games before joining the Wanderers for a fee of £115,000 in March 1995. Capable of playing at right-back or at the heart of the defence, he made his Wanderers' debut as a substitute in the League Cup Final against Liverpool at Wembley. He returned there the following month to play his part in the play-off win against Reading. After that, he missed very few games and scored a number of vital goals, perhaps none more enjoyable than the one against Spurs at White Hart Lane that earned the Wanderers their first away point in the Premiership. In 1996/97 he captained Bolton to the first division championship, after which he continued to be a rock in Bolton's back four. Capped 80 times by his country, Gudni postponed his impending retirement a couple of times before eventually calling it a day at the end of the 2002/03 season – having an outstanding final campaign as the club retained their top-flight status. Having appeared in 317 games for the Wanderers, he returned to Iceland to work as a lawyer.

IT'S A FARCE

The 1887/88 FA Cup competition became something of a farce with clubs spying on their opponent's players. Bolton met Everton in the first round and a goal from Bob Roberts seemed to have won the tie for the Wanderers but Everton successfully appealed against the qualification of Bolton's prolific marksman Bob Struthers, who proved ineligible by three days. The replayed game was drawn and a second replay also failed to produce a result before Everton won the fourth meeting 2-1. Everton were then beaten in the next round by Preston, who in turn went on to defeat Halliwell in the third round. Meanwhile, Bolton protested that Everton had fielded two professionals who were registered as amateurs. The FA found the Merseyside club guilty and suspended Everton for a month. Preston were brought back from the fourth round to face the Wanderers in the second, but North End showed little mercy in thrashing Bolton 9-1.

CELEBRITY FANS

Peter Kay ....Comedian, writer and producer
Vernon Kay......................................DJ and TV Presenter
Emma Forbes ....Children's TV Presenter
Amir Khan ....Professional boxer
Paul Nicholls ....Actor, formerly Joe Wicks in EastEnders

LEAGUE STATUS ALMOST LOST

In the final game of the 1889/90 season, Bolton needed to win the rearranged game against Burnley to stay out of the bottom four, who would need to seek re-election to the League. After leading 2-0, the Wanderers were pegged back by the Clarets and the game ended 2-2. With Aston Villa beating Cup winners Blackburn Rovers, the Wanderers finished fourth from bottom on goal average, the difference being one-hundredth in favour of Villa. At the League meeting, Bolton stated that the home defeat by Notts County had been by three goals and not four, thus placing them above Villa. The League settled the matter by saying that only Bolton and Burnley complied with the secretary's request for an official return of results and it was then agreed that Villa and Bolton stay in the League without having to go to re-election. This is the closest the club have come to losing their League status.

20 OR MORE LEAGUE GOALS IN A SEASON

Player	Goals	Season
Laurie Bell	23	1899/00
Sam Marsh	26	1904/05
Water White	24	1904/05
Albert Shepherd	26	1905/06
Walter White	25	1905/06
Albert Shepherd	25	1907/08
Billy Hughes	21	1910/11
Joe Smith	22	1911/12
Joe Smith	22	1912/13

George Lillycrop	24	1913/14
Joe Smith	29	1914/15
Frank Roberts	26	1919/20
Joe Smith	38	1920/21
Frank Roberts	24	1920/21
David Jack	24	1921/22
David Jack	24	1923/24
David Jack	26	1924/25
Joe Smith	24	1924/25
David Jack	24	1927/28
Harold Blackmore	30	1928/29
Harold Blackmore	30	1929/30
Harold Blackmore	27	1930/31
Jack Milsom	25	1932/33
Jack Milsom	23	1933/34
Ray Westwood	21	1933/34
Jack Milsom	31	1934/35
Ray Westwood	30	1934/35
Jack Milsom	20	1935/36
Ray Westwood	23	1937/38
George Hunt	23	1938/39
Willie Moir	25	1948/49
Nat Lofthouse	21	1950/51
Nat Lofthouse	22	1952/53
Nat Lofthouse	32	1955/56
Nat Lofthouse	28	1956/57
Nat Lofthouse	29	1958/59
Francis Lee	23	1964/65
Wyn Davies	21	1964/65
Francis Lee	22	1966/67
John Byrom	20	1969/70
John Byrom	20	1972/73
Neil Whatmore	25	1976/77
Frank Worthington	24	1978/79
John Thomas	22	1987/88
Andy Walker	26	1992/93
John McGinlay	25	1993/94
John McGinlay	24	1996/97

FIVE GOALS BUT RELEGATION LOOMS

At the end of the 1932/33 season, the Wanderers were relegated for the fifth time, going down to the second division along with Blackpool, as rivals Wolves and Leicester City both won. Victory over Leeds United on the final day was imperative for Bolton to have any hope of avoiding the drop and they did all they could before events elsewhere overtook them. Jack Milsom completed his hat-trick just before half-time and as the players left the field, the scoreboard showed that Wolves were losing at home to Everton. Bolton continued to dominate, running out 5-0 winners – the crowd even laughing as Milsom and Billy McKay missed open goals in the dying moments. However, the humour died down when it was realised that Wolves had won 4-2 and the club's 22 years in the top flight had come to an end.

THE TOPSHAM FISHERMAN

Bolton goalkeeper Dick Pym was born in the Devon village of Topsham and earned his living from the sea before joining nearby Exeter City in 1911. The Grecians were then members of the Southern League and Pym made 186 consecutive appearances for them before breaking his collarbone in an FA Cup tie against Watford. It was in July 1921 that the Wanderers secured his transfer after weeks of negotiation. Although the precise fee was never revealed, it was thought to be around the £5000 mark, which was a record for a goalkeeper. He made his debut in a 2-2 home draw with Preston North End and quickly settled into the team that won the FA Cup in 1923. His qualities were soon recognised and he played for the Football League XI in Belfast, yet despite his seafaring background, he was seasick on the crossing from Liverpool. In February 1925 he won the first of three full caps for England when he played against Wales at Swansea. He went on to win two more FA Cup winners' medals in 1926 and 1929, keeping clean sheets in all three Wembley appearances. The last survivor of the 1923 side, Pym played in 336 League and Cup games for the Wanderers before returning to live in Topsham.

FREIGHT ROVER TROPHY FINAL 1986

In Wanderers' opening game of the 1985/86 season's Freight Rover Trophy, they drew 2-2 at Stockport County, this after being two goals down with just three minutes to play. A 1-0 win at Crewe courtesy of a George Oghani goal put the Whites into the knockout stages of a competition that was to liven up the season. Tony Caldwell and Oghani got the goals that defeated Tranmere Rovers 2-1, whilst the same two players, along with Asa Hartford, were on the scoresheet in the Northern Area semi-final 3-0 win over Darlington at Feethams. Wigan Athletic were then beaten in the two-legged Northern Final to send the Wanderers to Wembley. On-loan keeper Dave Felgate's loan period had ended and manager Phil Neal had no choice but to play out-of-favour Simon Farnworth in goal. Bolton's opponents in the final were bogey side Bristol City and though Tony Caldwell hit the bar early in the game for the Wanderers it was the Ashton Gate club who took the trophy with a 3-0 win. Bolton's route to the final was as follows:

Round/scorers	Opposition	Score
Group ....Stockport County (a)............................		2-2
Came, Caldwell		
Group ....Crewe Alexandra (h)		1-0
Oghani		
Quarter-final ....Tranmere Rovers (h)............................		2-1
Caldwell, Oghani		
Semi-final..................Darlington (a).......................................		3-0
Oghani, Caldwell, Hartford		
Area Final 1 ....Wigan Athletic (a)		1-0
Caldwell		
Area Final 2 ....Wigan Athletic (h)		2-1
Oghani, Caldwell		
Final...........................Bristol City (n)*.....................................		0-3

*played at Wembley Stadium

Bolton's 1986 Freight Rover Trophy Final team: Farnworth, Scott, Phillips, Sutton, Came, Thompson (Bell), Neal, Oghani, Caldwell, Hartford, Green.

TRANSFER TRAIL

In chronological order, Bolton Wanderers' record purchases since the first £1000 signing have been as follows:

Player	Club	Year	Fee
Alf Bentley	Derby County	1911	£1000
David Jack	Plymouth Argyle	1920	£3500
Dick Pym	Exeter City	1921	£5000
Jack McClelland	Middlesbrough	1928	£6800
Jim Hernon	Leicester City	1948	£14,850
Harold Hassall	Huddersfield Town	1951	£27,000
Gareth Williams	Cardiff City	1967	£50,000
Terry Wharton	Wolverhampton Wanderers	1967	£70,000
Frank Worthington	Leicester City	1977	£90,000
Alan Gowling	Newcastle United	1978	£120,000
Neil McNab	Tottenham Hotspur	1978	£250,000
Len Cantello	West Bromwich Albion	1979	£350,000
Fabian de Freitas	Vollendam	1994	£400,000
Sasa Curcic	Partizan Belgrade	1995	£1.5m
Robbie Elliott	Newcastle United	1997	£2.5m
Dean Holdsworth	Wimbledon	1997	£3.5m
Nicolas Anelka	Fenerbahçe	2006	£8m

EGGS OR TAILS

During the summer of 1962, the Wanderers toured Greece, playing a number of the country's top sides including AEK Athens, Panathinaikos and Olympiakos. The festival of Easter is extended over a longer period in the Greek Orthodox and Byzantine Churches than in Western Churches and being an intensely religious country, the church's influence touches life in many ways. This was illustrated in the Wanderers' matches when the captains were given hard boiled eggs with which to toss for choice of ends! The eggs were coloured – one blue and one red – and it was astonished Bolton skipper Bryan Edwards who was handed an egg instead of the usual coin. The captains bang the two eggs together and the one whose shell is not cracked is deemed to have won the toss!

LOSS OF CONTROL

A crowd of 60,979 witnessed Bolton's disastrous fifth-round FA Cup tie against Manchester City at Burnden Park on 20 February 1937 – a match the visitors won 5-0. The Wanderers, who were struggling near the foot of the first division and were finding goals hard to come by, hadn't won a League game in ten attempts. Even so, they almost took the lead in the first minute but Frank Swift in the City goal tipped Jack Milsom's header over the bar. City did take the lead against the run of play just before the interval through Fred Tilson and though George Eastham hit the post for Bolton, City went 2-0 up courtesy of Alex Herd, who looked yards offside. Things started to get out of hand on the field and after Alf Anderson and Ernie Toseland were involved in a fracas, the Wanderers' Scottish winger received his marching orders. Then Bolton's Jack Tennant was fouled by Peter Doherty and the Bolton side demanded the offender's dismissal. When this wasn't forthcoming, with just a free-kick being awarded, Anderson appeared on the touchline trying to persuade his colleagues to leave the field! Eric Brook and Herd then put City 4-0 ahead before Eastham, resenting another poor refereeing decision, kicked the ball into the Embankment End. The crowd refused to return it and in time added on, Doherty scored City's fifth. Bolton's players had completely lost control with one of their players urging the referee to award a penalty kick against his own side.

ENGLAND PLAYED IN BOLTON SHIRTS

In April 1960, the Wanderers faced an England side at Burnden Park in a game lasting 20 minutes each way. The England side wore Bolton's home kit and won the game 2-0 with goals from Peter Broadbent and Joe Baker. For the record, the players wearing the Bolton shirts were: Ron Springett (Sheffield Wednesday), Jimmy Armfield (Blackpool), Ray Wilson (Huddersfield Town), Ronnie Clayton (Blackburn Rovers), Bill Slater (Wolves), Ron Flowers (Wolves), John Connelly (Burnley), Peter Broadbent (Wolves), Joe Baker (Hibernian), Ray Parry (Bolton Wanderers), and Bobby Charlton (Manchester United).

EARLY GROUNDS

Among the early grounds used by the Wanderers were the Park Recreation Ground and Dick Cockle's field on Pikes Lane opposite the Cross Guns public house. It was in 1874 that the newly formed Christ Church FC first played on these grounds but three years later, following a row with the Christ Church vicar, the club broke away under the name of Bolton Wanderers. In March 1881 the club moved to a ground just off Pikes Lane. The ground had two small stands and shallow banking around a cinder track but was notoriously very muddy and suffered from being at the foot of a hill from where an excellent free view was to be had! In February 1884, Athletic News reported that between 4,000 and 5,000 spectators had assembled on the slopes during Bolton's FA Cup replay against Notts County and an enterprising farmer charged them half the Pikes Lane entrance fee. The annual rent for the ground in 1888 had been £35 but five years later, with Bolton now enjoying higher gates, the landlord increased the rent to £175. The club began to look for a more suitable site and so Pikes Lane was last used in 1894/95. The Wanderers wound up League football at Pikes Lane in grand fashion. Cup finalists and eventual winners Aston Villa were beaten 4-3, Nottingham Forest were defeated 4-1 and on Good Friday, West Bromwich Albion were drubbed 5-0 with Peter Turnbull grabbing a second-half hat-trick.

WAR CUP WINNERS

Having accounted for Blackpool (Nat Lofthouse scoring all his side's goals in a 4-1 win at Bloomfield Road), Newcastle United and Wolves each over two legs in the qualifying rounds of the Football League War Cup in 1945, Bolton faced local rivals Manchester United in the two-legged Northern Final that was witnessed by almost 100,000 spectators overall. The first leg at Burnden Park saw Wanderers win 1-0 courtesy of another Lofthouse goal as he bundled keeper Jack Crompton and the ball into the net. A week later, Bolton received the Cup when they drew 2-2 at Maine Road with Malcolm Barrass netting his and Bolton's second goal in the final minute. The season was completed with a 2-1 win over Chelsea at Stamford Bridge before 45,000 spectators in the Football League War Cup, North v South Final.

BIRDMAN AT BURNDEN PARK

During an FA Cup fourth-round game with Arsenal at Burnden Park on Monday 31 January 1994 – which was televised live on Sky – play had to be suspended at a crucial stage when the attention of the whole stadium turned skywards. Both sets of players and the crowd of 18,891 saw someone buzz over the top of the stadium from a fan-powered parachute. The game was in its 29th minute when the incident took place but thankfully the 'birdman' disappeared to allow play to continue. The game ended all-square at 2-2 but Bolton won the replay 3-1.

THERE'S ONLY TWO...

The following names have been shared by two Bolton players.

Billy Hughes
William H Hughes 1908-1912; William Hughes 1948-1952
Jimmy Jones
James Jones 1919-1921 and James Jones 1937
Willie Morgan
William Morgan 1902 and William Morgan 1975-1979
Billy Russell
William Russell 1890-1891 and William Russell 1962-1964
George Taylor
George Taylor 1930-1939 and George T Taylor 1933-1937
Bob Taylor
Robert Taylor 1901-1906 and Robert Taylor 1997

LINESMEN OFFSIDE!

On 17 March 1973 in a game against Rochdale at Burnden Park – a match the Wanderers won 2-1 – both linesmen were situated on the Burnden side of the ground. The referee Ron Tinkler ordered both his linesmen to patrol the one line for the last half-an-hour of the game. Mr Butcher of Kendal made his pioneering move across the pitch to share the line with his colleague Mr Brown of Liverpool. The referee explained that he was unable to see his linesmen on the Manchester Road side due to the strong sun.

MANY HAPPY RETURNS

On 22 February 1933, Jack Milsom scored twice in a 4-1 win over Portsmouth at Burnden Park. It was the perfect present for Milsom, who was also celebrating his 26th birthday that afternoon. Here's a selection of Bolton players who have scored for the Whites on their birthday:

Player	Date	Opposition	Result
Bobby Langton	8 Sep 1951	Tottenham Hotspur	1-2
Willie Moir	19 Apr 1952	Manchester City	3-0
Nat Lofthouse	27 Aug 1955	Charlton Athletic	1-3
Nat Lofthouse	27 Aug 1958	Manchester City	3-3
Francis Lee	29 Apr 1967	Northampton Town	1-2
Neil Whatmore	17 May 1977	Bristol Rovers	2-2
Trevor Morgan	20 Sep 1988	Fulham	3-2
Andy Walker	6 Apr 1993	Stockport County	2-1
John McGinlay	8 Apr 1996	Chelsea	2-1
Ricardo Gardner	25 Sep 1999	Nottingham Forest	3-2

TV WHITES

(Malcolm) Darling Buds of May
(Gerry) Taggart
George (Oghani) and Mildred
Dixon of Dock (Scott) Green
(Rod) Wallace and Grommitt
Rumpole of the (Ian) Bailey
(Nathan) Blake's Seven
Alas (Joe) Smith and (Paul) Jones

NO RESPITE FOR THE CLARETS

Bolton's home game against Burnley on New Year's Day 1935, postponed due to the weather, was hastily arranged for the following day. The Wanderers – who went on to win promotion – thrashed the Clarets 7-0 with leading scorer Jack Milsom finding the net four times. The other scorers were Ray Westwood, Harry Goslin and George Eastham.

INTERNATIONAL APPEARANCES

The current holder of the club's international appearance record is Ricardo Gardner who broke the record on 21 November 2007 when playing for Jamaica v El Salvador. Jamaica won 3-0 with Gardner scoring twice. Below is the list of the top 10 international appearance makers while registered with the Wanderers.

Player	Country	Total
1. Ricardo Gardner	Jamaica	40
2. Jussi Jaaskelainen	Finland	34
2. Mark Fish	South Africa	34
4. Nat Lofthouse	England	33
5. Ted Vizard	Wales	22
6. Gudni Bergsson	Iceland	21
7. Per Frandsen	Denmark	18
8. Wyn Davies	Wales	16
9. Eddie Hopkinson	England	14
9. Jason McAteer	Republic of Ireland	14
9. John McGinlay	Scotland	14

THEY ALL COUNT

The 1972/73 season was an unforgettable promotion-winning campaign with the Wanderers lifting the third division championship. The home game against Rotherham United on 25th November 1972 saw one of the most bizarre goals ever seen at Burnden Park and proved to be the winner. The Millers had taken the lead before constant Bolton pressure finally told when John Byrom netted from point-blank range. Then, as the game seemed to be heading for a draw with only four minutes left, came an incredible goal that earned Bolton the points. Rotherham's keeper Jim McDonagh, later to join the Wanderers, seemed to have assumed that the ball had crossed the goal-line for a goal-kick. He placed the ball and turned to make his run-up. As he did so, Garry Jones ran up to slot it into an empty net with the referee waving play on. Despite great protests from the Rotherham players, the goal stood and Bolton won the game 2-1 to remain on top of the league.

THE EX FACTOR

Since the Premiership began in 1992, six Bolton players have scored against one or other of their former clubs in the league. They are:

Date	Player	Result
23 Dec 1995	Gudni Bergsson	Tottenham Hotspur 2 Bolton 2
25 Apr 1998	Neil Cox	Aston Villa 1 Bolton 3
13 Sep 2003	Kevin Davies	Bolton 2 Blackburn Rovers 2
24 Apr 2003	Kevin Davies	Southampton 1 Bolton 2
17 Dec 2005	Gary Speed	Everton 0 Bolton 4
2 Jan 2006	El Hadji Diouf	Bolton 2 Liverpool 2
25 Nov 2006	Nicolas Anelka*	Bolton 3 Arsenal 1
23 Dec 2006	Nicolas Anelka*	Manchester City 0 Bolton 2
14 Apr 2007	Nicolas Anelka	Arsenal 2 Bolton 1

two goals

TROTTERS WHO BECAME MANAGERS

The following Bolton Wanderers players went on to manager League clubs at the end of their playing careers: Sam Allardyce, Phil Brown, Dennis Butler, Owen Coyle, Martin Dobson, George Eastham, Bryan Edwards, Barry Fry, Matt Gillies, Stuart Gray, John Gregory, Asa Hartford, Dave Hatton, Colin Hendry, Charlie Hurley, David Jack, Warren Joyce, Brian Kidd, George Lillycrop, Nat Lofthouse, Neil McDonald, Willie Moir, John Napier, Phil Neal, Neil Redfearn, Peter Reid, Warwick Rimmer, Peter Shilton, Joe Smith, Dave Sutton, Ted Vizard, Mike Walsh, Frank Worthington and Charlie Wright.

SEMI-FINALS AT BURNDEN PARK

Burnden Park was the venue for four FA Cup semi-finals:

Date	Opponents	Result
23 Mar 1899	Liverpool v Sheffield United	4-4
23 Mar 1907	Everton v West Bromwich Albion	2-1
23 Apr 1966	Everton v Manchester United	1-0
26 Mar 1970	Leeds United v Manchester United	1-0

WHAT A SITTER!

It was the classic football trivia question that, alas, would never be asked: which club played in the first and last FA Cup Finals at the old Wembley Stadium? Answer: Bolton Wanderers. Having reached the semi-final in 2000, Bolton boss Sam Allardyce genuinely believed someone up there had decided to bestow sporting immortality upon the Whites. Then record-signing Dean Holdsworth smacked the ball against the foot of the Villa post in injury time before launching the most wayward of shots high over an open goal – a miss which has since become part of the town's folklore!

PLAY-OFF SUCCESS AT LAST!

Wanderers finally ended their play-off hoodoo in 1995 after three fruitless attempts – all in the third division: against Aldershot in 1986/87, Notts County in 1989/90 and Tranmere Rovers in 1990/91, when the club did reach Wembley but lost by a single goal to the Wirral outfit. After finishing third in the first division in 1994/95, Bolton travelled to Molineux to take on Wolves in the semi-final first-leg, a game which saw Peter Shilton became the club's oldest player but Bolton lost 2-1 with Jason McAteer grabbing the Wanderers goal. At Burnden Park, two goals from John McGinlay took the Whites into the Wembley final, where their opponents were Reading. Victory looked a distant dream following a lacklustre first half, especially after Bolton had gone 2-0 down in the opening quarter-of-an-hour. In fact, Reading were awarded a penalty in the 35th minute but a superb save from Keith Branagan kept the Wanderers in the game. In the second half, Bolton came out fighting, outclassing the Royals as they launched wave after wave of attack on the Berkshire club's goal. The Wanderers' determination was rewarded when Owen Coyle headed home 14 minutes from the final whistle and then, with just three minutes of normal time remaining, Fabian de Freitas equalised to take the game to extra time. Jason McAteer crossed for Mixu Paatelainen to head over Shaka Hislop to put Bolton 3-2 up and then de Freitas scrambled the ball past the Reading keeper after he had saved his first effort. Reading player-manager Jimmy Quinn reduced the arrears in the dying seconds. It was a most gutsy fightback by the Wanderers that clinched a place among football's elite.

CRICKET AT BURNDEN PARK

In May 1971 as part of the Wanderers' England international goalkeeper Eddie Hopkinson's testimonial, the Lancashire County Cricket team played an Eddie Hopkinson XI – Hoppy used to play for Heaton. Without doubt the star of the night was West Indian Test captain Clive Lloyd, whose domination saw Lancashire home by seven wickets. Lloyd hit a quickfire 44, an innings that included six sixes, a couple of them landing on the Burnden Stand roof, while his longest hit soared out of the ground!

PRISONERS OF WAR

During May 1945, German prisoners of war helped clear the Burnden Park paddocks of over 24,000 baskets – Ministry of Supply material – in readiness for the first leg of the League North Cup Final. Stacked neatly behind the stand, it made room for an extra 9,000 spectators who saw Nat Lofthouse score the game's only goal in a 1-0 defeat of Manchester United. The prisoners of war certainly didn't over-exert themselves with work – in fact, they even refused to work at all when it rained!

SEASON ENDS ON HIGH NOTE

Liverpool's visit to Burnden Park on the final day of the 1931/32 season saw the Merseyside club looking for revenge following an 8-1 defeat in a third-round Lancashire Cup tie. However, the Wanderers were 1-0 up after less than 30 seconds through Jack Milsom. The Bolton centre-forward netted again after five minutes before former Liverpool player Dick Edmed scored against his old club to make it 3-0 with barely seven minutes played. Danny McRorie pulled one back for the Reds after nine minutes, after which there was no further scoring in the first half. Early in the second half, Milsom completed his hat-trick and then scored a fine solo goal for his fourth and Bolton's fifth. Ray Westwood made it 6-1 before Fred Wilson netted what was his only league goal for the club. The rout was completed when Westwood headed home Milsom's cross. The crowd of just 9,209 were more than pleased to end a difficult season on a high note.

BOLTON'S BIGGEST WIN

Sheffield United must have taken leave of their senses when they agreed to switch their second-round FA Cup tie to Pikes Lane. Financially they were better off, of course, as Wednesday faced Accrington at their Olive Grove ground on the same day but the loss of home advantage left them with a mighty task, especially as the Wanderers had beaten Belfast Distillery 10-2 in the previous round. Pikes Lane was in a terrible state but it was difficult to see how the Blades could lodge a protest after agreeing to the change of venue. Davie Weir netted for Bolton after just 90 seconds and Walter Rushton thought he had doubled Wanderers' lead only to be ruled offside. Jack Parkinson in the Bolton goal was called upon to make a couple of saves before Weir scored his and Bolton's second moments later. James Brogan then finished a good move involving James Cassidy and Weir, before Cassidy netted a fourth. The heavy conditions prevented Bolton from playing their short-passing game but just before the interval Brogan scored Wanderers' fifth goal. Just after the restart, Cassidy made it 6-0 and every Bolton forward had chances to extend their side's lead before Cassidy, and then Weir, scored inside the space of a minute. Cassidy then scored the game's next two goals before Brogan smashed home the 11th and Weir the 12th. The Baker's Dozen was completed by full-back Bethel Robinson with the crowd shouting "you only need another seven to make the score".

FIRST CUP SUBSTITUTES

John Byrom was the first substitute used by Bolton in an FA Cup fixture – the prolific marksman replacing Dave Hatton in a fourth-round FA Cup tie against Arsenal at Burnden Park in February 1967. In the League Cup, the honour fell to Paul Fletcher in a second-round second replay against Rotherham United in September 1969, when he went on to replace John Ritson. In the Associate Members Cup (Freight Rover), Wayne Foster replaced Tony Caldwell in the first-round first leg defeat of Crewe Alexandra in January 1985. The club's first substitute in the Uefa Cup was club captain Kevin Nolan who came off the bench to replace Fabrice Fernandes in the game against Besiktas in October 2005.

SUPER JOHN MCGINLAY

John McGinlay played his early football with Nairn County before spending a season in New Zealand playing for Hanimex. On his return he was signed by then Gola League club Yeovil Town and after spending three-and-a-half seasons with the Somerset club joined Elgin City. His goalscoring achievements led to Shrewsbury manager Ian McNeill paying £25,000 for his services in February 1989. The following season he scored in both games against the Wanderers but in the summer of 1990 – after he had scored 31 goals in 68 games for the Shrews – he joined Bury for a fee of £175,000. While with the Shakers, McGinlay hit a hat-trick against the Wanderers at a rain-soaked Burnden Park in a 3-1 win for the Gigg Lane club but in January 1991, Bruce Rioch paid £80,000 to take him to Millwall. The London club reached the play-offs that season but in September 1992, Rioch, who was by now the Bolton boss paid £125,000 to bring him to Burnden Park. He made his debut in a 1-0 defeat at Leyton Orient but ended his first season with 22 goals as the Wanderers won promotion and reached the fifth round of the FA Cup. His goals in both matches against Liverpool and the penalty kick that beat Preston in the final game of the season endeared him to the hearts of Bolton fans. In 1993/94 he netted 33 goals to equal the post-war club record held by Nat Lofthouse and Andy Walker for total goals in a season. His record included hat-tricks against Charlton Athletic and Middlesbrough. In 1994 he won the first of 14 Scottish caps when he scored in a 2-1 win over Austria. McGinlay who netted another hat-trick in the 6-1 League Cup win over Spurs went on to score 118 goals in 245 games, including the last goal at Burnden Park, before joining Bradford City for £625,000 in November 1997.

PLASTIC

Four Football League clubs replaced their normal grass playing pitches with artificial surfaces at one stage or another – Queens Park Rangers were the first in 1981, Luton Town followed in 1985 and Oldham Athletic and Preston North End in 1986. The Wanderers never played on the Kenilworth Road or Boundary Park plastic and though they did better than most clubs when playing on the Deepdale version, they lost both games at Loftus Road, including a 7-1 mauling in 1981/82.

FA CUP FINAL 1926

This was the chance for the Wanderers to exact revenge over Manchester City for the defeat by their neighbours in the FA Cup Final of 1904. In one of the most sporting of finals, the game was closely and vigorously contested but it was 12 minutes from time before David Jack scored what transpired to be the game's only goal. Bolton had the upper hand in the first half but couldn't turn their superiority into goals, whilst City's best chance of the game came in the opening minute of the second half. Bolton again dominated proceedings and scored when a pass from Ted Vizard put Jack in the clear and he shot past Goodchild in the City goal. City had a chance to draw level in the closing minutes but Dick Pym, who had looked unbeatable throughout, made a fine save.

Round/ Scorers	Opponents	Score
Third	Accrington Stanley (a)	1-0
Jack		
Fourth	Bournemouth (a)	2-2
JR Smith, Jack		
Fourth (replay)	Bournemouth (h)	6-2
Boston, J Smith 2, Jack, JR Smith 2		
Fifth	South Shields (h)	3-0
J Smith (pen), Jack, JR Smith		
Sixth	Nottingham Forest (a)	2-2
Butler 2		
Sixth (replay)	Nottingham Forest (h)	0-0
Sixth (2nd replay)	Nottingham Forest (n)*	1-0
J Smith		
Semi-final	Swansea Town (n)**	3-0
Baggett, J Smith 2 (1 pen)		
Final	Manchester City (n)***	1-0
Jack		

*Played at Old Trafford, Manchester
** Played at White Hart Lane
***Played at Wembley Stadium

Bolton's 1926 FA Cup Final team: Pym, Haworth, Greenhalgh, Nuttall, Seddon, Jennings, Butler, Jack, JR Smith, J Smith, Vizard.

LAST CHRISTMAS DAY MATCH

A regular feature of the holiday League fixtures for many years was the Christmas Day match. These were, on a number of occasions, 11am kick-offs and continued until the late 1950s when the Football League decided to end matches on that day. The last Christmas Day match at Burnden Park was in 1954 against Tottenham Hotspur in the first division, when the north London club ran out 2-1 winners in front of a 25,978 crowd. Bolton did play in a further two games on Christmas Day, away to Manchester City in 1956 when they won 3-1 and at Everton in 1957 when the two sides played out a 1-1 draw.

LET THERE BE LIGHT

The first match to be staged under floodlights at Burnden Park was a friendly against the unbeaten Scottish League side Heart of Midlothian on 14 October 1957. A crowd of 21,058 witnessed a 1-1 draw, with Jimmy Wardaugh scoring for the Jam Tarts and Terry Allcock replying with a penalty. The referee for the occasion was Jack Clough, one in a line of notable Bolton referees. The cost of the lighting was put at £25,000 with the four pylons in each corner of the ground carrying 48 lights with an additional 170 lighting points provided in the stands, pay boxes, exit areas and car park. It was claimed that there was enough lighting to illuminate a path from Bolton to Blackpool. The lights, which were switched on by club chairman Harry Warburton, played host to further renowned visitors when, during November, the Russian Army side CDSA Moscow visited Burnden, the Wanderers recording their first floodlit victory – 3-0 before a crowd of 34,139. The floodlights were updated in 1975, whilst the whole towers and lamps were completely renewed in 1987.

GLITTERING PRIZES

FA Cup Winners 1923, 1926, 1929, 1958
Division One/Two Champions 1908/09, 1977/78, 1996/97
Division Two/Three Champions 1972/73
FA Charity Shield 1958
Sherpa Van Trophy Winners 1989

ELECTRICIAN LIGHTS UP BURNDEN

On 10 September 1983, Bolton part-time footballer and an electrician by trade, Tony Caldwell lit up Burnden Park with a personal feat of goalscoring in the third division match against Walsall. Signed from non-league club Horwich RMI for just £2,000, Caldwell equalled a club record for a first-class match set up by James Cassidy in the 13-0 defeat of Sheffield United in 1890 by scoring five times in Wanderers' 8-1 win. He grabbed a hat-trick in 27 minutes of first-half fury and though he added two more after the break, it could have been more! He began the blitz in the 18th minute by smashing home a chance set up by Warren Joyce and then four minutes later latched on to a long punt upfield by keeper Simon Farnworth. Within seconds Bolton were 3-0 up when Ray Deakin steered the ball into an empty net and then just on the stroke of half-time, Chandler's free-kick was flicked on by Simon Rudge for Caldwell to complete his hat-trick. On the hour mark, Neil Redfearn's shot was parried into the path of Caldwell for his fourth goal and the Bolton striker netted his fifth shortly afterwards as he met Gerry McElhinney's header at the far post. Simon Rudge struck from 25 yards to make it 7-0 before centre-half Peter Valentine scored his first goal for the club with perhaps the most spectacular – a 35 yard strike. In the dying seconds, Ally Brown tapped home a consolation for the Saddlers but it was enough to deny Bolton the chance of equalling their best-ever League victory.

ONE-GOAL WONDERS

As the saying goes, it only takes a second to score a goal. Sometimes though, it can take a good deal longer. Just look at the list of Bolton players, all of whom played over 100 league games for the club, but who only found the net once for the Whites.

Player	Games	Goal scored againt	Year
Syd Farrimond	365	v Norwich City (h)	1967
David Burke	175	v Chelsea (h)	1979
Matt Gillies	145	v Huddersfield Town (h)	1946
Eric Bell	102	v Wolverhampton Wanderers (h)	1955

THE AULD ENEMY

The Wanderers entered the Anglo-Scottish Cup for four consecutive seasons from 1976/77 to 1979/80. The qualifying stages took part during pre-season on a league basis with the qualifying clubs going through to face Scottish opposition over two legs. In 1976/77, Bolton qualified to face Partick Thistle in the knockout stages. The game at Burnden, in which myself and friends enjoyed a ride on the Thistle coach to direct Bertie Auld and his team to the ground, ended goalless. The tie was settled by a disputed Alan Hansen goal six minutes from time at Firhill. The Wanderers failed to qualify for the knockout stages in each of the next two seasons but did so in 1978/79 to face St Mirren. The Wanderers never recovered from the first 30 minutes of the game at Love Street. They were 4-0 down after 25 minutes and then on the half-hour mark, Len Cantello, who had been previously booked, was sent off. Frank Worthington pulled a goal back before half-time and then Polish winger Taddy Nowak hit a second for the ten men of Bolton to give the club some hope for the second leg. The Wanderers hit back at Burnden to level the aggregate score thanks to two fine Sam Allardyce goals but there was no further scoring and the game went into extra time. There were just two minutes remaining before the dreaded penalty shoot-out when Jim Bone netted for the Scottish outfit to knock the Wanderers out of the cup on a 5-4 aggregate.

QUICK-FIRE WEIR

The best-ever scoring sequence by a Bolton Wanderers player was achieved by English international David Weir during the 1889/90 season, when he netted 15 times in seven consecutive League and Cup matches. On 11 January, he netted twice in a 5-3 defeat of Notts County and followed this up a week later with four goals in the club's 10-2 FA Cup win over Belfast Distillery. Back in the League he netted in wins over Aston Villa, Stoke and Wolverhampton Wanderers – this latter game being played on 24 February. Squeezed in between these games was the club's second-round FA Cup tie against Sheffield United in which Weir netted another four in what is the club's record victory.

ATTENDANCES OVER 50,000

Attendance	Opponents	Date
69,912	Manchester City (FA Cup)	18 Feb 1933
65,419	Stoke City (FA Cup)	9 Mar 1946
65,295	Blackburn Rovers (FA Cup)	6 Mar 1929
60,979	Manchester City (FA Cup)	20 Feb 1937
58,692	Preston North End (FA Cup)	14 Feb 1959
57,207	Liverpool (FA Cup)	20 Feb 1965
56,667	Stoke City (FA Cup)	15 Feb 1958
56,306	Wolverhampton Wanderers (FA Cup)	1 Mar 1958
55,477	Manchester United (Division One)	1 Sep 1951
54,564	Everton (Division One)	15 Oct 1938
53,883	Portsmouth (FA Cup)	24 Feb 1954
52,568	Sheffield Wednesday (FA Cup)	17 Mar 1954
50,708	Manchester United (Division One)	11 Sep 1954
50,413	Everton (League Cup)	15 Feb 1977

SAFE HANDS... SOMETIMES

Since promotion in 1994/95, and despite their subsequent relegations in 1995/96 and 1997/98, Bolton have entrusted Premiership goalkeeping duties in their 342 games (to date) to just eight men:

Player	Dates	Apps	Sub
Jussi Jaaskelainen	1998/99-	250	0
Keith Branagan	1992/93-1999/00	65	0
Ali Al Habsi	2006/07-	10	0
Gavin Ward	1995/96-1998/99	9	2
Kevin Poole	2001/02-2005/06	4	1
Aiden Davison	1993/94-1996/97	2	0
Steve Banks	1998/99-2001/02	1	0
Andy Oakes	2004/05	1	0

Meanwhile, another goalkeeper, Ian Walker, has taken his place on the substitutes' bench for the Whites in the Premiership without being called into action, although appearing in Cup games for the club.

PREMIERSHIP BOUND KEITH BRANAGAN CELEBRATES WITH ALAN THOMPSON

WANDERERS ON TRIAL!

On 7 February 1927, Burnden Park hosted an England trial match. Three Bolton players were involved with Jimmy Seddon representing England and Dick Pym and Harry Nuttall playing for The Rest. A crowd of 14,002 saw The Rest run out winners 3-2.

PENALTIES

The club's first-ever penalty kick was awarded in a friendly match against Everton in January 1892; unfortunately Bolton captain Di Jones missed it! It was James Cassidy who had the distinction of scoring the club's first penalty, converting in a 2-0 win over Notts County at Pikes Lane the following March. Long-serving Jimmy Seddon, who went on to win three FA Cup winners' medals with the Wanderers, had the misfortune to give away a penalty for handball on his debut against Middlesbrough in February 1914. On Boxing Day 1924, the Wanderers travelled to Nottingham Forest where there were unprecedented scenes when the home side were awarded a penalty. No Forest player wanted to take the kick and the game was held up for a good five minutes. The club's normal penalty-taker, Harold Martin, had left the field injured and he returned to take the kick, which he converted to produce a 1-1 draw. Harold Hassall joined Bolton from Huddersfield Town and though he scored from the spot on seven occasions for the Wanderers, it was whilst he was with the Yorkshire club that he had the distinction of saving a penalty from the great Tom Finney – Hassall had to go in goal when the keeper was injured. Though Francis Lee was one of the game's most deadliest penalty-takers, it is John Thomas who holds the record for the most penalties scored in a season – eight in 1987/88.

CHAMPIONSHIP SEASON II - 1972/73

Wanderers made a good start to the season with a 3-0 home win over promotion favourites Bournemouth but early results were mixed. A 1-0 win over Chesterfield courtesy of an Alan Waldron goal took the Wanderers to the top and they remained there until the turn of the year. But as the club enjoyed a good FA Cup run, there were a number of slips in the League. The Wanderers eventually got back on track and showed good promotion form until the rearranged game against fellow promotion contenders and local rivals Blackburn Rovers at Burnden Park. A Derek Fazackerley goal gave Rovers a 1-0 win over a somewhat depleted Bolton side. Garry Jones and John Byrom, both of whom missed that Blackburn game, were still sidelined when the Wanderers travelled to Swansea City. The 17-year-old Neil Whatmore made his debut and scored twice in a 3-2 win. There followed a 2-0 defeat of Shrewsbury to give Bolton a five-point cushion at the top of the League. A Stuart Lee hat-trick against Halifax and a win over York ensured promotion and, following another triumph over already-relegated Brentford, the championship trophy was presented to skipper Warwick Rimmer.

Football League Division Three

	P	W	D	L	F	A	Pts
BOLTON WANDERERS	46	25	11	10	73	39	61
Notts County	46	23	11	12	67	47	57
Blackburn Rovers	46	20	15	11	57	47	55
Oldham Athletic	46	19	16	11	72	54	54
Bristol Rovers	46	20	13	13	77	56	53
Port Vale	46	21	11	14	56	69	53
Bournemouth	46	17	16	13	66	44	50
Plymouth Argyle	46	20	10	16	74	66	50
Grimsby Town	46	20	8	18	67	61	48
Tranmere Rovers	46	15	16	15	56	52	46
Charlton Athletic	46	17	11	18	69	67	45
Wrexham	46	14	17	15	55	54	45
Rochdale	46	14	17	15	48	54	45
Southend United	46	17	10	19	61	54	44
Shrewsbury Town	46	15	14	17	46	54	44
Chesterfield	46	17	9	20	57	61	43
Walsall	46	18	7	21	56	66	43
York City	46	13	15	18	42	46	41
Watford	46	12	17	17	43	48	41
Halifax Town	46	13	15	18	43	53	41
Rotherham United	46	17	7	22	51	65	41
Brentford	46	15	7	24	51	69	37
Swansea City	46	14	9	23	51	73	37
Scunthorpe United	46	10	10	26	33	72	30

LAWRENSON'S CLEAN SHAVE

Former Liverpool and Republic of Ireland star and now football pundit, Mark Lawrenson constantly tipped Bolton to be relegated during the course of the 2001/02 season and promised that if the Wanderers retained their place in the Premiership, he would have his moustache shaved off. Wanderers achieved top-flight survival and there was no way the Wanderers' supporters were going to let Lawrenson get away without paying the price – and so off came over a quarter-of-a-century's worth of facial hair: looking so much better, he hasn't regrown it, and at the time of writing the Wanderers are still in the Premiership.

KEEPING IT IN THE FAMILY

The following brothers, fathers and sons have all played for Bolton.

Brothers..*James and Richard Turner*
Having played in the club's reserves together on a number of occasions, the two played in all three FA Cup matches in 1888/89 with James netting a hat-trick in a 9-0 win over West Manchester.

Brothers...*Tom and John Buchan*
Tom Buchan, who joined the Wanderers from Blackpool in 1914, played in every position apart from full-back, even turning out as an emergency goalkeeper. His younger brother John also appeared for Bolton during the war.

Brothers..*Tommy and Ralph Banks*
Tommy was one of the great 'hard men' of the Bolton defence of the 1950s. Opportunities in the first team were few and far between as his brother Ralph occupied one of the full-back positions. Tommy Banks was a quality full-back with his best moments at Burnden coming towards the end of his career. In 1958 he collected an FA Cup winners' medal and appeared for England in the 1958 World Cup Finals in Sweden. Ralph was Tommy's senior by nine years. He lost his most promising years to the Second World War and made his last first-team appearance in the1953 FA Cup Final.

Father and Son .... *Bob and David Jack*
Bob Jack made his Bolton debut as a replacement for James Cassidy against Small Heath in September 1895. He could have little realised the influence he and his three sons David, Rollo and Donald were to have on Bolton Wanderers. Rollo joined the club from Plymouth in 1923 and stayed until 1929 making 31 League and Cup appearances, while Donald's appearances were restricted to the reserves. It was David Jack, most famous for scoring the first goal at Wembley, that made the biggest impression in Bolton colours.

Father and Son .... *Jocky and Billy Wright*
Jocky was signed from Clyde and was ever-present in the Wanderers first season at Burnden Park. His son Billy went into the team at the same time as another second generation Wanderer, David Jack. His breakthrough appeared to have come in the final game of the 1926/27 season when he netted a hat-trick in a 4-0 defeat of Huddersfield Town but this wasn't the case and his 154 appearances for the club were spread over 11 seasons.

THE REFEREE INSISTS

On 28 December 1889, the Wanderers defeated local rivals Burnley 6-3 on home soil in a scheduled Football League match. Prior to the game both sides had protested to the referee about the state of the ground, which was rock hard. But despite their reservations, the referee insisted that the game go ahead. The official did report the two club's disapproval of the conditions and so the League ordered a replay of the game. The rescheduled fixture was played after the planned final game of the season with the clubs playing out a 2-2 draw.

FIRST-EVER BURNDEN DISMISSAL

Towards the end of the game against Sheffield Wednesday at Burnden Park on 18 January 1902, with the Wanderers leading 3-0, Bolton's England international goalkeeper James Sutcliffe was given his marching orders for bad language directed at the referee after the official allowed a goal by the Owls that Sutcliffe claimed did not cross the goal-line. He was later suspended for 14 days.

THERE'S ONLY ONE ROBBIE SAVAGE

No, not the Welsh international who is currently plying his trade with Derby County, but Bolton's goalscoring hero on 7 May 1988 as the Wanderers won 1-0 at Wrexham to win promotion from the fourth division at the first attempt. Most Bolton fans thought the final day of the season would leave the Wanderers facing the nerve-wrenching play-offs but Savage's 68th minute strike coupled with Scunthorpe United's victory at Torquay clinched an unexpected return ticket to the third division for the Whites.

TRADESMAN'S ENTRANCE

With the traditional post-war career profession of a public house landlord having been superseded by media pundit or player's agent, here is a selection of slightly more individual ways in which former Bolton Wanderers players have earned a crust (sorry Wyn!) after hanging up their boots.

Player	Profession
Wyn Davies	Baker
Tony Dunne	Golf driving range proprietor
Wayne Entwistle	Meat Wholesaler
Syd Farrimond	Newsagent
Alan Gowling	Chemicals company manager
Dave Hatton	Estate agent
Dennis Stevens	Menswear shop owner
Neil Whatmore	Milkman

BOLTON ARMY

Following the outbreak of the Second World War, the whole of the Wanderers' team signed up for the Bolton Artillery and were later called up for service in the 53rd Bolton Artillery, being involved in fighting in the Middle East, Italian campaigns and the Dunkirk evacuation. Skipper Harry Goslin was killed in action in 1943 but the rest of the First-team squad survived and many returned to playing professional football after the hostilities.

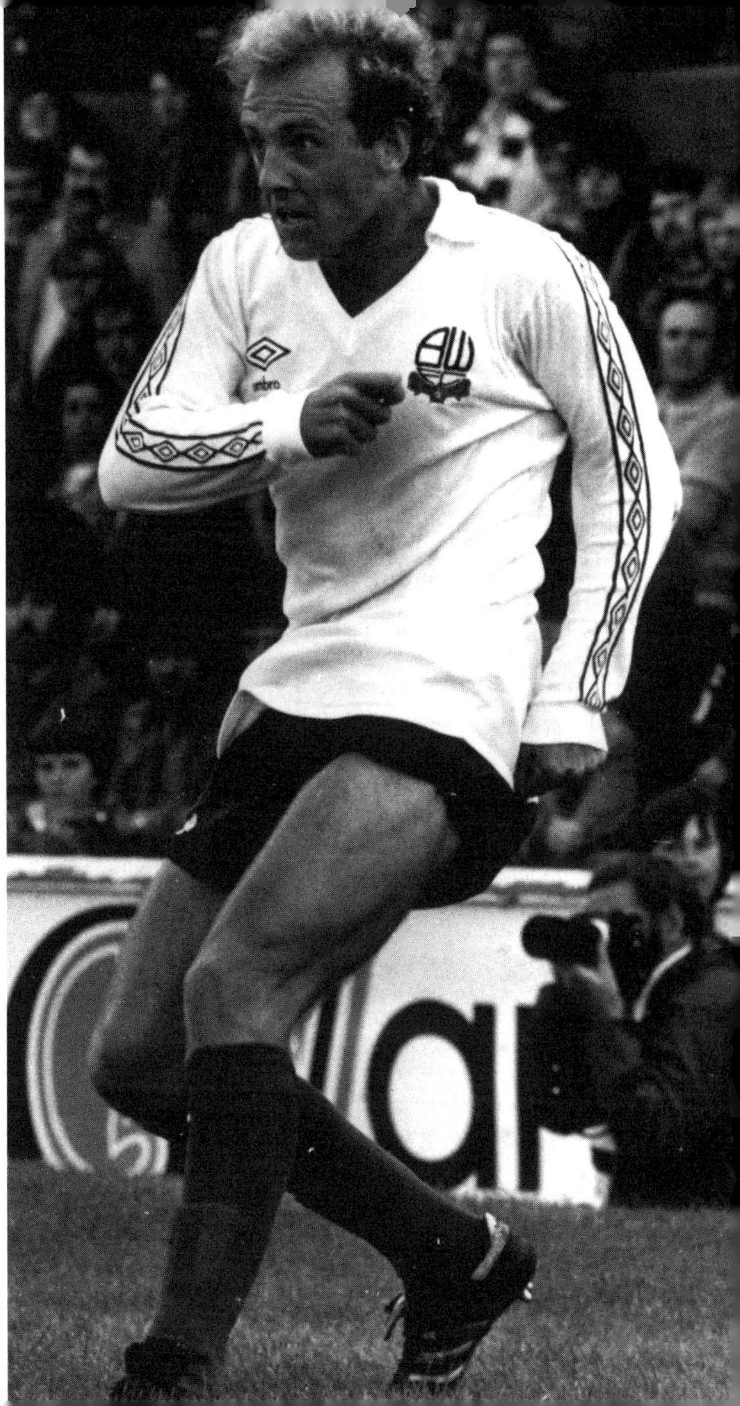

NEIL WHATMORE BECAME A MILKMAN AFTER HANGING UP HIS BOOTS

JACK THE LAD

Though David Jack is perhaps most famous for scoring the first goal in a Wembley Cup Final as the Wanderers beat West Ham United 2-0 in 1923, he contributed far more to the game than that. The son of the former Wanderer Bob Jack, he began his Football League career with Plymouth Argyle, where his father was the manager. Arsenal and Chelsea, with whom he had played during the First World War, wanted him, but he chose his home-town club and signed for the Wanderers in December 1920 for a then record fee of £3,500. He made his debut at inside-forward in a goalless draw at Oldham the following month and became a regular thereafter. For the next seven seasons he shared the goalscoring responsibilities with Joe Smith and was the club's top League scorer in five of them, with a best return of 26 goals in 1924/25. David Jack netted six of Bolton's seven FA Cup goals on the way to winning the trophy for the first time in 1923. A year later he won the first of four England caps while at Burnden. He scored the winner in the 1926 FA Cup Final but in October 1928, after having scored 161 goals in 324 games, he joined Arsenal for a then record £10,340 fee and went on to win both League Championship and further FA Cup winners' medals with the Gunners. He later managed Southend United, Middlesbrough and League of Ireland club Shelbourne. He worked as a sportswriter before retiring in April 1955. Jack also worked for the Inland Revenue as he had done during the early part of his career. He died in September 1958.

UNDEFEATED HOME RUNS

When Bolton met Chelsea at Burnden Park in the second division on 26 April 1911, in what was the penultimate game of that season, fans were expecting nothing less than victory. It was the Wanderers' nineteenth home League game of 1910/11 and they were unbeaten at Burnden Park. The Trotters won 2-0 courtesy of two Harold Hilton goals and in finishing runners-up to West Bromwich Albion, and so winning promotion to the first division, were unbeaten at home in a season for the first time since entering League football. The only other occasion when Bolton have gone through a season at home unbeaten was 1920/21 when they finished third in the first division.

FA CUP FINAL 1929

By beating Portsmouth in 1929, the Wanderers created something of a minor record in collecting the FA Cup for the third time in seven seasons, with all three finals played at Wembley Stadium. In the first-half, the side from Fratton Park did most of the attacking but Bolton's defence held firm and when half-time arrived, the game was still goalless. Six of the Bolton side had previous FA Cup Final experience – although goalkeeper Dick Pym was carrying an injury sustained in the run up to the big day. The Bolton breakthrough was late in coming, with Wanderers opening the scoring after 78 minutes, when Billy Butler netted with a tremendous shot that beat Pompey goalkeeper John Gilfillan. Harold Blackmore added a second to make the game safe and take the FA Cup back to Burnden Park yet again. Bolton's route to the 1929 FA Cup Final was as follows:

Round	Opposition	Score
Third	Oldham Athletic (h)	2-0
Gibson, Blackmore,		
Fourth	Liverpool (a)	0-0
Fourth (replay)	Liverpool (h)	(aet) 5-2
Butler, McClelland, Gibson, Blackmore 2,		
Fifth	Leicester City (a)	2-1
Seddon, Blackmore		
Sixth	Blackburn Rovers (a)	1-1
Blackmore		
Sixth (replay)	Blackburn Rovers (h)	2-1
Butler 2		
Semi-final	Huddersfield Town (n)*	3-1
Butler, Gibson, Blackmore		
Final	Portsmouth (n)**	2-0
Butler, Blackmore		

* played at Anfield
** played at Wembley Stadium

Bolton's 1929 FA Cup Final team: Pym, Haworth, Finney, Keen, Seddon, Nuttall, Butler, McClelland, Blackmore, Gibson, Cook.

FIRST TELEVISED LEAGUE MATCH

On 10 September 1960, the Wanderers took part in the first-ever Football League match to be televised in full, when they travelled to Bloomfield Road, Blackpool, for a first division clash. However, as an initial television showpiece, it was a poor advertisement for League football, lacking even the cup-tie tension of a typical Lancashire 'derby' struggle. From start to finish it was scrappy in the extreme with Bolton manager Bill Ridding describing Wanderers' performance as the worst they had given in his time in charge. Even so, the Wanderers did win 1-0 with the only goal being scored by Freddie Hill just before the final whistle!

LATE FINISHES

Bolton's play-off final game against Tranmere Rovers at Wembley Stadium on Saturday 1 June 1991 is the latest date for the finish of any Wanderers season in peacetime. If play-offs are excluded, Bolton's latest finish to a normal league season was 17 May in seasons 1965/66 and 1976/77 when they travelled to Ipswich Town and Bristol Rovers, losing 1-4 and drawing 2-2, respectively. During the Second World War many curious things occurred, not least in professional football: among them the continuance of the 1940/41 and 1944/45 seasons right into June. Thus Bolton's last competitive match in the 1940/41 season was on 7 June at Oldham Athletic while on 2 June 1945 they won 2-1 at Chelsea.

CAN YOU SPELL THAT?

Some of the more elongated formal names of Bolton's recent players have included:

Full Name	Aka
Diouf El Hadji Ousseynou	El Hadji
Giannakopolous Stilianos	Stelios
Jaidi Radhi Ben Abdelmajid	Radhi
Okocha Augustine Azuka	Jay Jay
Timotian-Samarani Adranik	Teymourian

FAMILIAR FACES

Since the two sides first met home and away in the inaugural season of 1888/89 in the first division, Bolton Wanderers' most frequent opponents in the Football League have been Aston Villa. Pikes Lane was the venue for the first home game and of course the two teams subsequently met at Burnden Park and the Reebok. Bolton's top ten most-played opponents are:

	P	W	D	L	F	A
Aston Villa	142	53	34	55	227	224
Blackburn Rovers	136	56	31	49	212	214
Everton	128	33	30	65	169	211
West Bromwich Albion	128	47	39	42	210	185
Sunderland	122	44	28	50	175	201
Preston North End	118	43	30	45	170	172
Wolverhampton Wanderers	114	44	21	49	171	204
Derby County	112	38	17	57	171	207
Birmingham City	110	43	31	36	176	151
Burnley	110	39	29	42	153	152

FROZEN STIFF

A modern-day record of sorts was established during the 1978/79 season when Bolton beat Manchester United 3-0 at home on 22 December 1978, then due to bad weather didn't play at home again until 64 days later, beating Chelsea 2-1 on 24 February. In that time the team played three away games, drawing at Middlesbrough and Norwich City and were knocked out of the FA Cup by Bristol City.

LADIES FOOTBALL AT BURNDEN PARK

In April 1921, almost 30,000 spectators packed into Burnden Park to see a football match between a Bolton Ladies' team assembled by Bolton's Welsh international winger Ted Vizard's wife and Dick Kerr's XI, which formed four years previously. Dick Kerr's team were instrumental in raising over £35,000 for local charities, whilst the proceeds for this match were in aid of the Bolton and District ex-Servicemen's fund. For the record, Dick Kerr's XI won 8-0.

UPPERS AND DOWNERS

Since Bolton took their place in the Football League, the club has enjoyed
– and endured – no fewer than 24 movements between the divisions.

Season	Move
1898/99	Relegated (Div 1 to 2)
1899/00	Promoted (Div 2 to 1)
1902/03	Relegated (Div 1 to 2)
1904/05	Promoted (Div 2 to 1)
1907-08	Relegated (Div 1 to 2)
1908/09	Promoted (Div 2 to 1)
1909/10	Relegated (Div 1 to 2)
1910/11	Promoted (Div 2 to 1)
1932/33	Relegated (Div 1 to 2)
1934/35	Promoted (Div 2 to 1)
1963/64	Relegated (Div 1 to 2)
1970/71	Relegated (Div 2 to 3)
1972/73	Promoted (Div 3 to 2)
1977/78	Promoted (Div 2 to 1)
1979/80	Relegated (Div 1 to 2)
1982/83	Relegated (Div 2 to 3)
1986/87	Relegated (Div 3 to 4)
1987/88	Promoted (Div 4 to 3)
1992/93	*Promoted (Div 2 to 1)
1994/95	Promoted (Div 1 to Prem)
1995/96	Relegated (Prem to Div 1)
1996/97	Promoted (Div 1 to Prem)
1997/98	Relegated (Prem to Div 1)
2000/01	Promoted (Div 1 to Prem)

* Post Premiership

FIRST OVERSEAS SIDE

On 28 October 1899, the first overseas side to visit Burnden Park was
the Kaffirs. A crowd of 1500 saw the South African touring side beaten
13-3. Hugh Morgan scored four goals in what was a 'farcical game',
even goalkeeper John Sutcliffe managed to find the net!

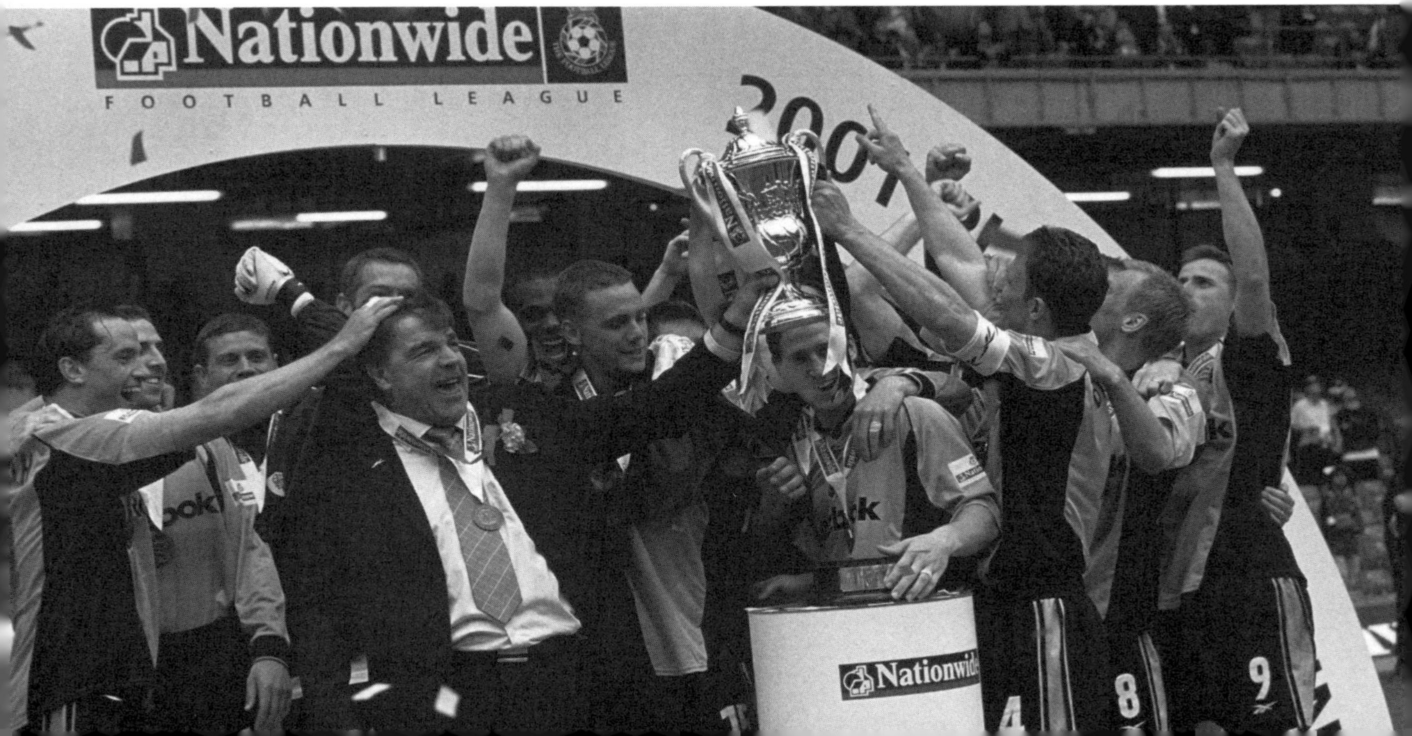
Nationwide
FOOTBALL LEAGUE
Nationwide

SEMI-FINALS

Bolton Wanderers have played in 15 FA Cup semi-final games – including replays at 14 different venues.

1889/90	Sheffield Wednesday	lost 1-2	Perry Barr
1893/94	Sheffield Wednesday	won 2-1	Fallowfield
1895/96	Sheffield Wednesday	drew 1-1	Goodison Park
1895/96	Sheffield Wednesday	lost 1-3	Town Ground
1903/04	Derby County	won 1-0	Molineux
1914/15	Sheffield United	lost 1-2	Ewood Park
1922/23	Sheffield United	won 1-0	Old Trafford
1925/26	Swansea Town	won 3-0	White Hart Lane
1928/29	Huddersfield Town	won 3-1	Anfield
1934/35	West Bromwich Albion	drew 1-1	Elland Road
1934/35	West Bromwich Albion	lost 0-2	Victoria Ground
1945/46	Charlton Athletic	lost 0-2	Villa Park
1952/53	Everton	won 4-3	Maine Road
1957/58	Blackburn Rovers	won 2-1	Maine Road
1999/00	Aston Villa	drew 0-0*	Wembley

lost 1–4 on penalties aet

MCWANDERERS!

During the club's early days in the Football League, the Wanderers had on their books a number of Mc's recruited from north of the border. These included players such as Marshall McEwan, Jim McGeachan, John McNee and Jim McKie. The tradition continued in earnest after the Second World War with a number of Mc's starring for the Whites (although not all were from Scotland). Here's a selection:

Player	Seasons	Apps	Goals
Billy McAdams	1960/61 to 1961/62	52	29
Don McAllister	1969/70 to 1974/75	176/1	2
Jason McAteer	1992/93 to 1995/96	139/6	15
Jim McDonagh	1976/77 to 1982/83	274	1
Gerry McElhinney	1980/81 to 1984/85	125/2	2
John McGinlay	1992/93 to 1997/98	230/15	118

BRAZIL NUTS?

Brazil's World Cup team came to Bolton for their pre 1966 World Cup Finals practice and drove straight into a 'who plays where' controversy. The World Cup favourites thought they were to train on the Burnden Park pitch but the Wanderers' management had already decided that the club's training facilities at Bromwich Street would be used. There was then a meeting between Bolton officials and Brazil officials which ended with the Bolton chairman, Ted Gerrard, offering the visitors the full use of Burnden Park and all its facilities. The Brazilians went away but then came back and said they preferred Bromwich Street! Their only stipulation was that they could have use of the Burnden medical room and that Coca-Cola should be served to the team, not tea.

HAT-TRICK TREBLE

In December 1910, the Wanderers played three second division games at Burnden Park. All were won – Huddersfield Town (3-1) Birmingham (5-1) and Leicester Fosse (6-2) – with centre-forward Billy Hughes scoring a hat-trick in each game. In the first game of the New Year, the Wanderers defeated Barnsley 4-0 but Hughes only managed to score twice!

YOUNG KIDS ON THE BLOCK

After a run of seven League and Cup games without a win and relegation from the second division staring the Wanderers in the face, a team with an average age of just 20 was fielded against promotion-chasing Sheffield United on 16 January 1971. Though Jimmy Meadows had been appointed manager the previous day, the side containing seven teenagers had been selected by caretaker boss Nat Lofthouse. The Burnden Babes fell behind after just 95 seconds to a John Tudor goal before Ian Seddon levelled the scores on 19 minutes. The Whites then had a Paul Fletcher goal disallowed and Ronnie Phillips hit the post but 11 minutes from time, Fletcher scored the goal that sent the crowd wild. Sadly, this proved to be a false dawn – the last 16 games of the season went by without a win and the club were relegated to the third division for the first time in their history.

LOCAL RIVALS

The games against our friends and neighbours from Bury have never been short on excitement. The very first game between the two clubs in the League was on 7 September 1895 at Bury, where Bolton won 3-0. The Wanderers biggest winning margin against Bury at Burnden Park in the League is 4-0, which came in December 1905, thanks to two goals from Walter White and one each from Sam Marsh and Marshall McEwan. Two seasons later, the Shakers recorded their best result at Burnden, winning 6-3 on the opening day of the season, with Harold Tufnell netting a hat-trick for Bury and Albert Shepherd doing likewise for Bolton. In the FA Cup, Bolton and Bury have been drawn together on four occasions with the Wanderers coming out on top each time. The first was in 1894 when a goal from James Cassidy was enough to settle the last Cup-tie at Pikes Lane. In 1990/91, Bolton beat Bury over two-legs in the play-offs (1-0 at Burnden and 1-1 at Gigg Lane) and though they came under the auspices of the League, they certainly took the form of cup-tie football. In previous two-legged games between the clubs, it is Bury who have had the upper hand – in the 1947 Lancashire Cup semi-final and the 1986/87 League Cup competition. In fact, it was in the League Cup of 2002/03 when the two sides last met with Bury winning 1-0 at the Reebok!

LEAGUE CUP FINAL 1995

In the previous season, the Wanderers had made a name for themselves with some stirring performances in the FA Cup but during 1994/95, it was to be the Coca-Cola Cup that earned the club more national headlines. Premiership sides Ipswich Town, West Ham United and Norwich City were all accounted for as the club got through to the two-legged semi-final against another first division club, Swindon Town. Trailing 2-1 after the first leg at the County Ground, the Wanderers again made things difficult for themselves by allowing the Robins to take the lead at Burnden Park, only to hit back with three later goals from Jason McAteer, Mixu Paatelainen and John McGinlay to reach the final for the first time. Bolton's opponents at Wembley were Liverpool and it was the Reds who drew first blood after 37 minutes when Steve McManaman drilled a low shot past Keith Branagan. The exciting England international added a second in the 67th minute after cutting inside Scott Green and curling a right-foot shot out of Branagan's diving reach. Before the restart, Icelander Gudni Bergsson came on for his Bolton debut and within two minutes he was involved in Bolton's goal. His cross was headed straight back to him from Neil Ruddock. The substitute returned the compliment with a header to Paatelainen who nudged the ball in the direction of Alan Thompson. The former Newcastle player controlled the ball on his chest, pivoted and blasted a spectacular left-footer into the top right-hand corner of David James' goal. The Bolton fans sensed their never-say-die heroes had a chance of taking the game into extra time but sadly it wasn't to be. Bolton's route to the final was as follows:

Round	Opposition	Score
Second (first leg)	Ipswich Town (a)	3-0
McAteer, McGinlay, Thompson		
Second (second leg)	Ipswich Town (h)	1-0
Sneekes		
Third	Sheffield United (a)	2-1
Paatelainen, Scott og		
Fourth	West Ham United (a)	3-1
McGinlay 2 (1 pen), Lee		
Fifth	Norwich City (h)	1-0
Lee		
Semi-final (first leg)	Swindon Town (a)	1-2
Stubbs		
Semi-final (second leg)	Swindon Town (h)	3-1
McAteer, Paatelainen, McGinlay		
Final	Liverpool (n)*	1-2
Thompson		

played at Wembley Stadium

Bolton's 1995 League Cup Final team was: Branagan, Green (Bergsson), Phillips, McAteer, Seagraves, Stubbs, Lee, Sneekes, Paatelainen, McGinlay, Thompson.

GRIM CHRISTMAS

There was little festive cheer for Bolton fans in 1902 as they saw their team lose 5-1 at Liverpool on Christmas Day. On Boxing Day, the Wanderers travelled to Sheffield United, where they were thrashed 7-1. The mince pies tasted no better after Bolton's third game in as many days when they visited Merseyside a second time. On this occasion they played Everton but they were beaten yet again, this time 3-1. Oh well, surely the new year would bring better luck! Wrong! In their first match of 1903 Bolton went down 1-0 at home to Grimsby Town and then lost their next two games to Sheffield Wednesday and West Bromwich Albion, respectively.

GREATEST-EVER GOAL

If ever one moment of genius deserved to win a game of football, it came after 38 minutes of the Bolton versus Ipswich Town game at Burnden Park on 23 April 1979, when Frank Worthington scored the most amazing of goals. Sadly, the Portman Road side won the game 3-2 but even so, Worthington, in front of England boss Ron Greenwood and the television cameras, stole the show. When the ball came to the Bolton striker he had only one thing in mind and that was to hit the target. Back to goal, he juggled the ball with his head, twice with his left foot, then lifted it over his head before pivoting and firing a shot on the volley past Paul Cooper's left hand.

MILESTONE GOALSCORERS

The following players have made history by scoring the following League goals for the club:

1000th............................ Walter White v Bury (home 3-1) 9 Mar 1907
2000th........ Billy Wright v West Bromwich A (away 1-1) 16 Oct 1926
3000th........................ Nat Lofthouse v Wolves (home 3-2) 6 Dec 1947
4000th................ Peter Deakin v Sheffield W (home 3-0) 28 Dec 1963
5000th.............. John Thomas v Grimsby Town (home 1-2) 3 Oct 1981
6000th..... Arnar Gunnlaugsson v Bradford C (away 2-2) 23 Aug 1998

GOAL NUMBER 6000: ARNAR GUNNLAUGSSON

HOME FROM HOME

Aside from Burnden Park and the Reebok, the venue at which
Bolton Wanderers have earned the most Premiership points is The
Valley. Here's the complete record of how and where the Whites
have earned their points on the road since promotion in 1994/95,
up to the time of writing.

Opposition	Frequency	Record	Points
Charlton Athletic	6 visits	4 wins 1 draw 1 defeat	13
Blackburn Rovers	9 visits	3 wins 3 draws 3 defeats	12
Southampton	6 visits	3 wins 2 draws 1 defeat	11
Leeds United	5 visits	3 wins 1 draw 1 defeat	10
Aston Villa	8 visits	2 wins 3 draws 3 defeats	9
Manchester City	7 visits	3 wins 0 draws 4 defeats	9
Everton	9 visits	2 wins 1 draw 5 defeats	7
Manchester United	8 visits	2 wins 1 draw 5 defeats	7
Tottenham Hotspur	8 visits	2 wins 1 draw 5 defeats	7
Chelsea	8 visits	1 win 2 draws 5 defeats	7
Leicester City	3 visits	1 win 2 draws 0 defeats	5
Middlesbrough	7 visits	1 win 2 draws 4 defeats	5
Portsmouth	5 visits	1 win 2 draws 2 defeats	5
Coventry City	2 visits	1 win 1 draw 0 defeats	5
Crystal Palace	2 visits	1 win 1 draw 0 defeats	5
Newcastle United	9 visits	1 win 2 draws 6 defeats	5
West Ham United	7 visits	1 win 2 draws 4 defeats	5
Sunderland	4 visits	1 win 1 draw 2 defeats	4
Arsenal	9 visits	0 wins 3 draws 6 defeats	3
Birmingham City	5 visits	1 win 0 draws 4 defeats	3
Ipswich Town	1 visit	1 win 0 draws 0 defeats	3
Reading	2 visits	1 win 0 draws 1 defeat	3
Watford	1 visit	1 win 0 draws 0 defeats	3
Wigan Athletic	2 visits	1 win 0 draws 1 defeat	3
Wolves	1 visit	1 win 0 draws 0 defeats	3
Derby County	3 visits	0 wins 1 draw 2 defeats	1
Fulham	7 visits	0 wins 1 draw 6 defeats	1
Liverpool	9 visits	0 wins 1 draw 8 defeats	1
Sheffield United	1 visit	0 wins 1 draw 0 defeats	1

Wimbledon ....2 visits .... 0 wins 1 draw 1 defeat 1
Barnsley.............................1 visit........... 0 wins 0 draws 1 defeat........ 0
Nottingham Forest...........1 visit........... 0 wins 0 draws 1 defeat........ 0
Queens Park Rangers.......1 visit........... 0 wins 0 draws 1 defeat........ 0
Sheffield Wednesday........2 visits .... 0 wins 0 draws 2 defeats 0

LAST GAME AT BURNDEN PARK

The Wanderers signed off in style as the curtain came down on 102 years of football at Burnden Park. Their opponents, Charlton Athletic, certainly made it difficult and Mark Kinsella's spectacular 18th-minute 25-yard shot that whistled past Keith Branagan silenced the 22,030 crowd. However, no-one was going to spoil this party and after Alan Thompson, who changed his boots at half-time, equalised in the opening minute of the second half, it was all one-way traffic. Gerry Taggart crashed home an unstoppable volley that put the Bolton fans in sight of the victory the occasion merited before two late goals from ace marksman John McGinlay, the first a penalty, put the result beyond doubt and gave the Wanderers a fighting chance of achieving the unique double of 100 points and 100 league goals. Bolton manager Colin Todd sent up Gudni Bergsson, McGinlay and Taggart to receive the 108-year-old trophy, formerly the prize of the English League champions, while Nat Lofthouse and chairman Gordon Hargreaves dug up the centre spot in a symbolic transfer of the Burnden spirit to take to the new Reebok Stadium. Bolton's team in the last-ever game at Burnden Park was: Branagan, Bergsson (McAnespie), Fairclough, Taggart, Phillips, Johansen (Sheridan), Frandsen, Thompson, Sellars, Blake (Paatelainen), McGinlay.

MIDDLE NAMES

A selection of uncommon middle names that Bolton Wanderers players have admitted to: Malcolm Williamson Barrass, Harry Woodgate Greenhalgh, David Howcroft Hatton, John Oldfield Higgins, David Bone Nightingale Jack, George Beanland Lillycrop, Ernie Rixon Phythian, John Barclay Picken, Jack Woolfall Rimmer, Billy Bullock Wright.

NEUTRAL TERRITORY

Burnden Park was used as a neutral ground for FA Cup matches on a number of occasions. In 1899, the ground was awarded its first FA Cup semi-final, a replay between Liverpool and Sheffield United and the following November, Burnden was the venue for a Football League representative game against the Irish League. In April 1901, the FA Cup Final replay between Spurs and Sheffield United took place. Commonly known as 'Pie Saturday' this is covered in more detail elsewhere in the book. During the 1960s, Burnden was honoured with selection for two FA Cup semi-finals. In 1966 Everton and Manchester United played their tie whilst four years later a second replay between Manchester United and Leeds United took place. The Wanderers themselves have had to replay on a neutral ground a number of times:

Date	Opponents	Venue	Round	Score
11.2.1897	Grimsby Town	Bramall Lane	Two	3-2
13.2.1915	Millwall	Ewood Park	Two	4-1
15.3.1926	Nottingham Forest	Old Trafford	Six	1-0
25.2.1935	Tottenham Hotspur	Villa Park	Five	2-0
16.1.1939	Middlesbrough	Elland Road	Three	0-1
9.2.1953	Notts County	Hillsborough	Four	1-0
23.2.1959	Preston North End	Ewood Park	Five	1-0
12.2.1973	Cardiff City	The Hawthorns	Four	1-0
23.2.1976	Newcastle United	Elland Road	Five	1-2
18.10.1977	Fulham*	St Andrew's	Three	2-1

League Cup

FA Cup semi-finals and finals, and League Cup finals were also played on neutral grounds and have their own entry elsewhere in the book.

FIRST THREE-POINTER

Bolton had to wait until the fifth game of the 1981/82 season before picking up their first three points for a win after the Football League upped the reward for a win from two points in a bid to stop teams hanging on for draws. It came courtesy of a 2-0 win at Derby County with Chris Thompson and Gerry McElhinney on target.

THE LION OF VIENNA

Whenever football conversation turns to 'real' centre-forwards, then there is one name that is certain to be mentioned – Nat Lofthouse. He was big and strong, just as most centre-forwards were supposed to be but in the age of the maximum wage he was loyal to his only club, Bolton Wanderers. He was proud of his ability and status but always remained a member of the local community. Bolton born and bred, Nat's father was head horsekeeper for Bolton Corporation and Nat the youngest of four sons. His first proper game of football was not a happy one; pressed into service as an emergency goalkeeper, the 11-year-old debutant suffered the indignity of picking the ball out of the net seven times! But that match gave him an insight into what organised football was all about and on his own request he was included in the school team – at centre-forward. Size was the determining factor then but he made steady progress and when he earned his debut for Bolton Schools XI against Bury, he scored all seven goals in a 7-1 win. It was the Mayor of Bolton, himself a club director, who asked the young Lofthouse to join the Wanderers. He was signed as a 14-year-old amateur in 1939 and made his first team debut in 1940. Bury were again the victims but this time Lofty was content with just a brace of goals. He still had to prove himself and wartime football was not easy. Bevin Boy Lofthouse's Saturdays went like this: up at 3.30 am, catching the 4.30 tram to work, eight hours down the pit pushing tubs; collected by the team coach; playing for Bolton. But work down the mine toughened him physically and the caustic humour of his fellow miners made sure he never became arrogant about his success on the field. When the war finished, the chance to play alongside established professionals returning from the forces gave Lofthouse the final confidence he needed and he was a regular in the league side from the resumption in 1946. Goals flowed regularly, attracting favourable press comment as it became obvious that Lofthouse had international potential. In 1949 he scored four goals for an FA XI against the Army and the following year he was selected for the FA summer tour of Canada. The call to full international honours came the following November against Yugoslavia. The game was played at Highbury and despite the presence of ex-ballet dancer Vladimir Beara in goal and 6ft 4in Ivan Horvath at centre-half, both England goals in a 2-2 draw were scored by Lofthouse. Within a year he was established as England's centre-forward and from October 1951 to November 1953 he didn't miss a game for his country. One of those 18 matches against Austria in May 1952 was to give Lofthouse the famous nickname 'Lion of Vienna'. With the scores level at 2-2, Lofthouse, having scored England's opening goal, was put through on goal by Tom Finney's shrewd pass. With the desperate defence in pounding pursuit, Lofthouse slid the ball under the advancing Musil before being felled by a crunching tackle. It was a great triumph but as he regretfully said: "I never saw the ball enter the Austrian net for the best goal of my life." Strangely, his international career seemed to be over after the 1955/56 season, one of his best – 32 league goals in 36 games including four in a 6-0 win over Birmingham City and four international goals in five games. The 1958 World Cup came and went, then Lofthouse was surprisingly recalled to the England team for two games and scored his 30th international goal (equalling Finney's newly-established record) with a powerful shot against Russia. He was named Footballer of the Year in 1953 – the trophy being presented the night before the Cup Final in which Bolton were beaten 4-3 by Blackpool. Lofthouse took to the pitch needing a goal to complete a remarkable record of scoring in every round. He did not have to wait long! It was 1958 before Lofthouse gained an FA Cup winners' medal as Bolton beat Manchester United 2-0. He scored both goals that day – the second seeing United keeper Harry Gregg hit the net as hard as the ball after Lofty's charge caught him off the ground. Before nagging injury ended his playing career in the early 1960s, he had scored over 300 goals – 255 in 452 league games, 30 in 51 Cup games, 30 in 33 internationals, and he even scored a hat-trick in each half for the Football League against the League of Ireland at Molineux. After a spell out of the game, when he kept a pub, he returned to the Wanderers in 1968 as manager. The experiment was not a success and though he was replaced briefly, he was then re-appointed. He left the club in 1971 on Jimmy Armfield's appointment but returned to become executive club manager and later president to continue his devotion to Lancashire's oldest club.

BOLTON LEGEND: NAT LOFTHOUSE AT THE REEBOK

PELE FOR BOLTON?

Following the sacking of manager George Mulhall in 1982, Wanderers' new chairman Terry Edge told an astonished news conference of the incredible plan to land the former Brazilian star – the biggest name in world football. Club secretary Des McBain was due to fly to America to set up a meeting with the soccer superstar but the following day, the legendary Pele rejected the chance of becoming the new player-manager at Burnden Park. Pele said he was flattered but because he was under a long-term contract with Warner Communications, he wouldn't consider Bolton's invitation.

BOLTON'S NUMBER ONE

During his 14-year Bolton career, the Whites' legendary England international goalkeeper Eddie Hopkinson (1956/57 to 1969/70) played 578 games for the club, keeping 138 clean sheets. His enduring quality helped him see off four rivals, all of whom played at least one game for the Wanderers during Hopkinson's undisputed reign as number one.

Goalkeeper	Matches played	Clean Sheets
Joe Dean (1955/56 to 1959/60)*	15	3
Johnny Bollands (1959/60)	13	1
Alex Smith (1962/63 to 1967/68)	20	4
Alan Boswell (1969/70 to 1970/71)+	23	5

Also played for Bolton before Hopkinson's debut
+ Also played for Bolton after Hopkinson's retirement

A DIFFERENT KIND OF HAT-TRICK

One of the strangest hat-tricks concerning the Wanderers is the fact that they entertained Birmingham on three consecutive New Year's Day fixtures from 1924 to 1926, winning two and drawing one. Joe Smith obviously enjoyed this fixture, netting the Wanderers goal in a 1-1 draw in 1924, scoring twice in a 3-0 win in 1925 and then hitting a hat-trick in a 5-3 success in 1926.

NUMBER 12: TWO FIRSTS

Substitutes weren't introduced to the English game until the start of the 1965/66 season. The first appearance of a substitute in the whole of the Football League came at Burnden Park when Charlton Athletic's Keith Peacock came on during Wanderers' 4-2 win. Gordon Taylor became the first-ever Bolton substitute to come off the bench when he replaced John Napier in the eleventh game of the season, a 3-2 home defeat by Southampton. Fans had to wait until the seventh game of the 1969/70 season for the first goalscoring substitute when Gordon Taylor scored the opening goal in a 2-0 defeat of Birmingham City.

WINNING RUN

In 1904/05, the Wanderers won 11 matches on the trot. The run started on 5 November 1904 when Gainsborough Trinity were beaten 5-1 at Burnden Park. They then went on to record victories against Lincoln City (home 4-1), Burton United (home 7-1), Liverpool (home 2-0), Doncaster Rovers (away 4-0), Port Vale (away 2-1), West Bromwich Albion (home 2-1), Lincoln City (away 2-0), Leicester Fosse (away 4-2), Bristol City (home 3-1), and Burnley (home 2-1) before on 3 January 1905, the Wanderers went down 4-2 at home to Manchester United. The Wanderers ended the season as runners-up to Liverpool, winning promotion to the first division.

PIE SATURDAY

In 1901, Burnden Park was chosen as the venue for the Cup Final replay between Tottenham Hotspur and Sheffield United. In eager anticipation of a bumper crowd – the first game was watched by 114,815 at Crystal Palace – the town's tradesmen brought in massive stocks of pies and souvenirs. But the day turned into a disaster, for Bolton railway station was in the process of being rebuilt and the railway company refused to offer cheap-day excursion tickets. A lot of merchandise went to waste that day, as only 20,470 turned up. Known for years afterwards in Bolton as Pie Saturday, one firm of pie-makers alone produced 13,000 while another prepared half-a-ton of sandwich meat. At night, 2d pies were being remaindered at three for 2d and later given away!

CENTURION GOALSCORERS

The following 13 players have all scored 100 or more goals for Bolton Wanderers.

Nat Lofthouse 285
Joe Smith 277
David Jack 161
Jack Milsom 153
Ray Westwood 144
Willie Moir 134
John Byrom 130
Harold Blackmore 122
Neil Whatmore 121
John McGinlay 118
Francis Lee 106
James Cassidy 101
Dennis Stevens 101

TRUE COLOURS

In the Football Field of 24 October 1881, the Wanderers were called 'the Reds'. Later that season they wore jerseys of 'scarlet and white quarters', decorated with an embroidery representing the coat of arms of the borough. In 1884/85 the Wanderers tried out a new and startling kit for the home match against Sheffield Wednesday – 'a loose white shirt with red spots' – this displaced the earlier salmon pink that figured in the FA Cup fourth-round tie against Notts County at Trent Bridge on 19 January 1884. In May 1886, the Wanderers sported 'lily jerseys' and in December, blue and white, while in 1890 something akin to the present scheme appears to have been favoured. Up until recently, the Wanderers have in the main worn white shirts and navy shorts though in 1969/70 they did play in all white – as today – but new boss Jimmy Armfield reverted back to the traditional white shirts and navy shorts. In recent years, with the advent of sponsors, the players have sported a variety of light blue, yellow, maroon and white shirts – all popular, but perhaps none more so than the club's away strip of red and blue stripes.

ALL WE ARE SAYING IS GIVE US A GOAL

The Wanderers' worst run in front of goal is five games – a dismal run which first occurred in 1897/98 and was repeated in 1989/90. In this latter season, the run began on 16 March 1989 with a 2-0 defeat at Wigan Athletic and continued until 3 April 1989 when Tony Philliskirk netted twice in a 3-0 home win over Reading. The five games in which the Whites failed to score were:

Date	Result
16 March 1989	Wigan Athletic 2 Bolton Wanderers 0
20 March 1989	Bolton Wanderers 0 Crewe Alexandra 0
24 March 1989	Bolton Wanderers 0 Brentford 1
27 March 1989	Leyton Orient 0 Bolton Wanderers 0
31 March 1989	Chester City 2 Bolton Wanderers 0

UTILITY PLAYERS

A utility player is one of those particularly gifted footballers who can play in several or even many different positions. One of the club's earliest utility players was Tom Buchan, who between 1914 and 1923 played in every position except full-back. He even turned out as an emergency goalkeeper in a 4-2 reverse at Stockport during the war years and in a 3-2 win on the same ground two years later. Don Howe made his debut in 1936, taking over the right wing position from Jack Rimmer in a goalless draw at Anfield. By the end of the season he had played in every forward position, later proving himself capable of filling in any position before settling at wing-half and becoming club captain. Johnny Wheeler and Derek Hennin were wing-halves who in the 1950s showed their versatility by turning out as an emergency centre-forward, each scoring a hat-trick! Wheeler hit three in Bolton's 4-0 defeat of Blackpool in January 1953, whilst Hennin's treble came in the match against Aston Villa on Good Friday 1958 as the Wanderers won by the same scoreline. As the game has progressed, much less attention came to be paid to the implication of wearing a certain numbered shirt, although Peter Nicholson and Julian Darby were versatile enough to wear every outfield shirt.

BOBBY MOORE OFF!

During the 1976/77 season, the Wanderers were involved in a controversial League Cup replay with Fulham. The Londoners were leading 2-1 when in the fifth minute of injury time, Mike Walsh equalised to make it 2-2. A couple of minutes later, the referee blew for full-time and was immediately surrounded by Fulham players remonstrating at his time-keeping. The outcome was that England's 1966 World Cup winning captain Bobby Moore was sent off. This decision resulted in the Fulham players appearing to walk off in support. It needed an ultimatum from the official to get the Cottagers to return for extra-time, which remained goalless. The Wanderers then won the third meeting 2-1 at the neutral venue of Birmingham City's St Andrew's ground. Later that season when Fulham visited Burnden Park for a league game it resulted in crowd segregation at the ground for the first time.

ONE-CAP WONDERS

Eight players have won just the one cap for England while playing their football for Bolton. They are:

Player	Date	Opposition
James Turner	13 March 1893	Wales
Billy Bannister	22 March 1902	Ireland
Albert Shepherd	7 April 1906	Scotland
Billy Butler	12 April 1924	Scotland
George Eastham	18 May 1935	Holland
Harold Hassall	11 November 1953	Northern Ireland
Johnny Wheeler	2 October 1954	Northern Ireland
Michael Ricketts	13 February 2002	Holland

COUNT THE GOALS

Bolton's record win at home was a 13-0 victory against Sheffield United on 1 February 1890 in an FA Cup second-round tie. Away from home it was a 7-1 victory at Aston Villa on 26 December 1914 in a first division match.

WYN THE LEAP

Wyn Davies had a spell with Llanberis before joining his home-town club Caernarfon. From there he entered League football with Wrexham and scored 26 goals in 67 games, including a hat-trick on his last appearance for the Robins as Hartlepool United were beaten 10-1. In March 1962 he joined the Wanderers in a transfer deal worth £20,000 in cash plus Ernie Phythian, who was reportedly valued at £10,000. He made his debut in a 5-1 defeat at Wolverhampton Wanderers and after that missed very few games in four-and-a-half seasons with the club. After winning the first of 34 Welsh international caps in 1964, 'Wyn the Leap' as he was popularly known, scored his first hat-trick for the club in a 3-0 win over Southampton. He ended the 1964/65 season as the club's top scorer with 25 goals in 38 games. His performances for the Wanderers led to his name being linked with a number of top clubs and in October 1966, after scoring 74 goals in 170 games, he joined Newcastle United for £80,000. He helped the Magpies win the Inter Cities Fairs Cup before winding down his career with the two Manchester clubs, Blackpool, Crystal Palace, Stockport County and Crewe Alexandra.

FIRST HAT-TRICK

The man honoured with scoring the first league hat-trick for Bolton Wanderers is David Weir, who achieved the feat on 22 December 1888 in a 4-1 victory over Accrington – at the Pikes Lane ground – in the inaugural season of the Football League.

WHO'S IN GOAL THIS WEEK?

Bolton boss Phil Neal helped to set a club record in season 1991/92 by selecting no fewer than five different goalkeepers at one time or another during the campaign. Welsh international Dave Felgate headed the list with 25 appearances, followed by fellow Welsh keeper, on-loan Andy Dibble (13), Kevin Rose (4) and other on-loan keepers Andy Maxwell (3) and Gerry Peyton (one appearance). New manager Bruce Rioch wasn't impressed by any of the quintet and, in the close season, signed Keith Branagan from Millwall.

WE WERE SO RUDELY INTERRUPTED

One immediate effect of Britain's formal declaration of war against Germany on 3 September 1939 was the immediate suspension of competitive football fixtures. That meant that the opening games of the 1939/40 season were expunged from the records including Bolton's three games in the first division.

Date	Result
26 August 1939	Chelsea 3 Bolton Wanderers 2
28 August 1939	Stoke City 1 Bolton Wanderers 2
2 September 1939	Bolton Wanderers 2 Portsmouth 1

When the Football League programme resumed after the war, the 1939/40 fixture list was resurrected with the Wanderers faring better by winning all three games.

Date	Result
31 August 1946	Chelsea 3 Bolton Wanderers 4
5 September 1946	Stoke City 1 Bolton Wanderers 2
7 September 1946	Bolton Wanderers 1 Portsmouth 0

Appearing in both the opening game of 1939 and 1946 against Chelsea were no fewer than five players: Stan Hanson, Don Howe, Harry Hubbick, Ted Rothwell and Ray Westwood. Of the other six players who played in the 1939 game against Portsmouth, three remained on the Bolton staff, appearing later in that 1946/47 season, whilst George Taylor, who played his last game in 1945, became the club's coach, Danny Winter joined Chelsea and Harry Goslin lost his life fighting in the Second World War.

CHARITY BEGINS AT HOME

On 6 October 1958, the Wanderers, who were the FA Cup holders, met League Champions Wolverhampton Wanderers in the FA Charity Shield match at Burnden Park. A crowd of 15,239 saw the Trotters win 4-1 with goals from Lofthouse 2, Neville Bannister and Freddie Hill (penalty).

FOREIGN OPPONENTS

There have been as number of overseas visitors to Burnden Park down the years, the first being a South African touring team known as 'the Kaffirs' in October 1899 and they were defeated 13-3! A crowd of 1,500 witnessed what was described as a farcical game with the Wanderers running up an 8-1 half-time advantage, including a goal by keeper John Sutcliffe. The club's first overseas tour came in May 1909 with a visit to the Netherlands, where they were advertised as the second division champions of Great Britain. The highlights of the five-game tour which all ended in victory, was a 3-0 defeat of Dutch champions Sparta and a 10-1 success over Dordrecht. On the club's next tour, to Germany, they again saved the best till last with a 12-0 win over the German Association in Breslau with Billy Hughes scoring five goals. After winning the FA Cup in 1923, the club broke new ground by visiting France and Switzerland and in 1929 after another FA Cup success, the Wanderers were invited to open a new 65,000 all-seater stadium in Barcelona. Unfortunately Bolton went down 4-0 to the Cataluna club in front of the Spanish king! Visits to Scandinavia in the early 1950s were replaced by visits to organised tournaments and in 1958 Bolton after beating Flamengo de Rio of Brazil in Paris on the toss of a coin after a 1-1 draw and a 3-3 draw on penalties, lost to Racing Club Paris in the final. After finishing 4th in division one in 1958-59, Bolton travelled to South Africa but despite playing on hard baked surfaces after the rain and mud of a Football League season, they won eight of their ten games. Bolton continued to beat all-comers at Burnden Park and in fact, the first time they lost at home to foreign opposition was August 1979 when Ajax of Amsterdam won 3-1.

CHAMPIONSHIP SEASON III – 1977/78

Bolton started the season in tremendous form, winning six and drawing one of their opening seven games, including a 2-0 defeat of relegated Sunderland – a result which propelled them to the top of the second division. An inspired signing in the form of Frank Worthington – who scored on his debut against Stoke – saw an improvement in the overall strength of the squad. Even players of the calibre of Paul Jones and Peter Reid, who had been out of action through injury and suspension, found it difficult to reclaim their places in the side. A Roy Greaves' goal in a

1-0 win over Spurs, the club's nearest rivals, saw Bolton go four points clear at the top. Despite victories over Notts County and Blackpool over Christmas, the club lost two games in the space of three days at Millwall and at home to Burnley – allowing Spurs to go top. The two clubs also drew each other in the FA Cup with Bolton winning after a replay. This result gave the club a great fillip and they went to Sheffield United and won 5-1. Just one defeat in eight games following the club's fifth-round FA Cup exit at Middlesbrough saw Bolton maintain their challenge but a 1-0 defeat against Spurs at White Hart Lane saw the north London club take over the leadership of the division. A Worthington goal on a wonderful night at Ewood Park confirmed the Wanderers' promotion and a goalless home draw against Fulham on the final day of the season was enough to clinch the second division title.

Football League Division Two

	P	W	D	L	F	A	Pts
BOLTON WANDERERS	42	24	10	8	63	33	58
Southampton	42	22	13	7	70	39	57
Tottenham Hotspur	42	20	16	6	83	49	56
Brighton & Hove Albion	42	22	12	8	63	38	56
Blackburn Rovers	42	16	13	13	56	60	45
Sunderland	42	14	16	12	67	59	44
Stoke City	42	16	10	16	53	49	42
Oldham Athletic	42	13	16	13	54	58	42
Crystal Palace	42	13	15	14	50	47	41
Fulham	42	14	13	15	49	49	41
Burnley	42	15	10	17	56	64	40
Sheffield United	42	16	8	18	62	73	40
Luton Town	42	14	10	18	54	52	38
Orient	42	10	18	14	43	49	38
Notts County	42	11	16	15	54	62	38
Millwall	42	12	14	16	49	57	38
Charlton Athletic	42	13	12	17	55	68	38
Bristol Rovers	42	13	12	17	61	77	38
Cardiff City	42	13	12	17	51	71	38
Blackpool	42	12	13	17	59	60	37
Mansfield Town	42	10	11	21	49	69	31

LEAGUE CUP FIRST

The club first took part in the competition in 1960/61 with Hull City being their first opponents. The initial game took place at Hull's Boothferry Park ground, where the teams played out a goalless draw. The replay at Burnden Park nine days later saw the Wanderers run out 5-1 winners with Freddie Hill and Bill McAdams each finding the net twice, whilst the other goal came from winger Brian Birch. A crowd of just 10,781 watched the first League Cup tie. In the next round, Nat Lofthouse netted a hat-trick as the Whites beat Grimsby Town 6-2 and they followed this up by beating Darlington 2-1. The club's interest in that season's competition ended in the fourth round with a 2-0 home defeat at the hands of Rotherham United.

ALL-TIME APPEARANCES

Eddie Hopkinson....... 1956-1969........ 578
Roy Greaves.............. 1965-1980........ 575
Alex Finney............... 1922-1936........ 530
Warwick Rimmer ...... 1960-1974........ 528
Bryan Edwards .... 1950-1965........ 518
Ted Vizard .... 1910-1930........ 512
Paul Jones................. 1971-1983........ 506
Nat Lofthouse............ 1946-1960........ 503
Roy Hartle .... 1953-1966........ 499
Joe Smith .... 1909-1927........ 492

WHAT A FUSSY REF!

During the 1967/68 season, Bolton entertained local rivals Blackburn Rovers a week after being beaten by Nottingham Forest at the third-round stage of the FA Cup. The Wanderers bounced back to form and were leading Rovers 2-1 courtesy of two Gareth Williams strikes when referee Maurice Fussey blew for full-time. However, only 85 minutes of the game had been played and after his mistake had been pointed out to him by a linesman, a further five minutes was played with the Wanderers holding on for victory.

LONG SERVICE

Nat Lofthouse, the club's most illustrious personality, has been with the club since 1939, first as a player, then as coach after his retirement through injury, and later manager. His association ended in 1972 but six years later he returned to become manager of the Executive Club. In December 1985 he took charge again, albeit for one game and in 1986 he capped what has been almost a lifetime's service (63 years at the time of writing) by becoming the club's president. Charles Foweraker was persuaded to become secretary pro tem, when Tom Mather was called up in 1915. After guiding the club through the war years, he was appointed secretary-manager in 1919. He was in charge during the 1920s when the Wanderers won three FA Cup Finals at Wembley. He was awarded the Football League's long-service medal in recognition of more than 21 years in the Wanderers' employment. In August 1944, Foweraker retired through ill-health, having completed 49 years' continuous service with the club. He had entered football in a part-time capacity in 1895, acting as a checker when Burnden Park opened. Walter Rowley went to Bolton from Oldham Athletic in 1912 and served the club well until he was forced to retire through injury in May 1925. He was appointed coach to the reserves and first-team coach at the outbreak of war. In 1944 he was promoted to secretary-manager but six years later resigned due to ill-health and was awarded life membership of the club for services rendered during his 38 years at Burnden Park. George Taylor served the Wanderers for over 50 years as a player, coach and scout and even after retirement still worked for the backroom staff on a part-time basis. Bill Ridding's association with Bolton Wanderers began in 1946 when he was appointed manager, a position he didn't relinquish until August 1968. At the time of his departure he was second only to Matt Busby as the League's longest-serving manager. In recent years Sam Allardyce, who had two spells at the club as a player, also spent almost eight years as manager. There are also a number of Bolton players who have given long service to the club. Ted Vizard, who made 512 first team appearances, making his last in 1931 before taking charge of the 'A' team, gave almost 23 years' service to Bolton. Other players include Joe Smith (1908-1927), Jimmy Seddon (1914-1932), David Stokes (1902-1920), Roy Greaves (1965-1980), Alex Finney (1922-1937), Warwick Rimmer (1960-1974), and Bryan Edwards (1950-1965).

YOU'LL NEVER BEAT THE WANDERERS

Clubs that Bolton have never lost to in Football League games are:

	P	W	D
Darwen	4	4	0
Halifax Town	6	3	3
Hereford United	4	3	1
Loughborough	2	2	0
Rochdale	6	2	4

The only team the Wanderers have never beaten is:

	P	W	D
Scunthorpe United	6	5	1

FIRST GAME AT THE REEBOK

Years in the planning, months in the building, 90 minutes of football was never going to do justice to the work that went into the magnificent Reebok Stadium. In the event, the game that heralded the dawn of a new era was a disappointing anti-climax. The Reebok staged its first-ever game when the Wanderers entertained Everton in the Premiership and Sky TV cameras were there to record the historic event. Fans paid silent tribute to Diana, Princess of Wales, before the game, the crowd of 23,131 solemnly observing a one-minute silence before kick-off. Unfortunately, the game failed to match the event and disaster struck when Robbie Elliott, Bolton's recent £3.5m signing from Newcastle United, was stretchered off with a broken leg. Though the game was goalless, the Wanderers did actually get the ball over Neville Southall's goal-line when in the 54th minute Gerry Taggart's header looped over the Welsh international keeper and dropped over the Everton line before full-back Terry Phelan hacked it away. To everyone's amazement, the referee waved play on and though Nathan Blake spurned a good chance, there wasn't another worthwhile scoring effort from either side. Bolton's team in the first game at the Reebok was: Branagan, Phillips, Bergsson, Taggart, Elliott (McAnespie), Pollock, Frandsen (Johansen), Thompson, Sellars, Beardsley (McGinlay), Blake.

FREE BEER

In September 1982, Burnden Park was the venue for their sponsor's Ingersoll Rand's attempt to break the record for the biggest 'shout' for a round of drinks. The existing record of 1,222 was the target but there were only 136 takers for the free beer! The organisers were left with more than 200 gallons of beer on their hands and the best part of £1,000 unspent.

THE INSPIRATIONAL JOE SMITH

A magnificent centre-forward and inspirational captain, Joe Smith began his career as an amateur with Newcastle St Luke's in the Staffordshire League before joining the Wanderers. He made his league debut in a 2-0 defeat at West Bromwich Albion in April 1909 before establishing himself as a first team regular in 1910/11. His performances for the Wanderers in the years up to the First World War led to him winning the first of five full caps for England in February 1913 in a 2-1 defeat of Ireland. Smith played in 51 wartime games for the Wanderers, scoring 48 goals, including six against Stoke in September 1916 as Bolton won 9-2. He 'guested' for Chelsea along with Ted Vizard while serving in the RAF and in 1918 they both helped the Stamford Bridge club win the London v Lancashire Cup Final. He was Bolton's most consistent scorer until Nat Lofthouse and his 38 goals, which included hat-tricks against Middlesbrough (home 6-2), Sunderland (home 6-2) and Newcastle United (home 3-1) in 1920/21 – still a club record. In 1923 came Joe Smith's greatest honour when he was the first FA Cup Final captain to receive the trophy at Wembley. Three years later he lifted the Cup again but his career at Bolton was coming to an end. After heading the Wanderers' league-scoring charts for the sixth time, Smith, who had scored 277 goals in 492 games, joined Stockport County in March 1927 for £1,000. For the Edgeley Park club he scored 61 goals in 69 league games but in 1929 he joined Darwen and had a spell at Manchester Central before becoming manager of Reading. Four years later he became Blackpool's manager, a position he held until April 1958, when he was the longest-serving manager in the Football League. He guided the Seasiders to their best-ever League position and to the 1948, 1951 and 1953 FA Cup Finals.

WHEN WILL WE WIN AGAIN?

During the course of the 1901/02 and 1902/03 seasons, the Wanderers went 26 league games without a win – the worst run in the club's history. Having failed to win any of their last four games of the 1901/02 campaign, in which the club finished twelfth in the first division, they then failed to win any of their opening 22 games of the 1902/03 season. The record-breaking run was eventually ended on 17 January 1903 when goals from Jimmy Hanson, Sam Marsh and Bob Taylor helped Bolton beat Notts County 3-1. Though they then won five consecutive games, it didn't prevent them finishing bottom of the division.

FIRST INTERNATIONALS

Bolton's first international players for the home nations and the Republic of Ireland were:

England ....Kenny Davenport...v Wales.........14 Mar 1885
Scotland ....Alex Donaldson......v Wales.........28 Febr 1914
Wales...........................Jack Powell..............v England ....17 Mar 1884
Northern Ireland ....Billy Hughes...........v Wales...........7 Mar 1951
Republic of Ireland...Charlie Hurley .....v Hungary..... 8 Jun 1969

FAMOUS GUEST PLAYERS

During the Second World War, clubs playing in regional league competitions were allowed to use guest players – usually servicemen in the Armed Forces who were stationed nearby. The most distinguished player to 'guest' for the Wanderers was the Preston North End and England forward Tom Finney, who made his debut for Wanderers against Burnley at Turf Moor, going on to score seven goals in ten games. Bill Shankly, future legendary Liverpool manager, also promised to play for the Wanderers but he was transferred with his unit to Scotland and played for East Fife. However, the following season he did manage to play in two games for the Wanderers whilst on leave, scoring in the 3-0 defeat of Oldham Athletic.

TAXI PLEASE!

During the 1919/20 season, the first peacetime campaign after the First World War, football was faced with further problems due to railway strikes. A number of the lower league games were postponed on account of the visiting team being unable to get to their destination. For the game at Derby County, the Wanderers arrived at the Baseball Ground by means of a number of taxis. Bolton won 2-1 with goals from Joe Smith and Jack Feebury, whilst in goal for the Rams was James Kidd, who had been sold to County four days earlier by the Wanderers.

WORLD CUP WHITES

Over the years there have been ten Bolton Wanderers players who have represented their country at the World Cup Finals.

Year	Player	Country
1954	Nat Lofthouse	England
1958	Tommy Banks	England
1994	Jason McAteer	Republic of Ireland
1998	Mark Fish	South Africa
1998	Per Frandsen	Denmark
2002	Youri Djorkaeff	France
2002	Stig Tofting	Denmark
2006	Jared Borgetti	Mexico
2006	Hidetoshi Nakata	Japan
2006	Radhi Jaidi	Tunisia

HAPPY DAYS

During the course of the 1968/69 season, Bolton supporters were invited to submit their ideas as to the name of the club's new mascot. Nat Lofthouse and club captain Dave Hatton judged the entries and came up with 'Happy'. The club shop became the 'Happy' shop and there was a 'Happy' Burnden Beat in full swing where record requests and messages could be sent. During the following season, a two-foot high model in wood of the mascot was stolen from a cartoon exhibition at Smithills Coaching House – the search for 'Happy' was on.

DISASTROUS DEBUTS

Llanelli-born goalkeeper Dai Davies, who later went on to win three full international caps and appear in 137 League and Cup games for the Wanderers, certainly didn't have the best of debuts and things got even worse on his next appearance. His first game between the posts for Bolton came on Christmas Day 1902 when the Wanderers went down 5-1 at Liverpool. Having kept his place for the Boxing Day trip to Sheffield United, Davies then proceeded to let in even more goals as Bolton lost 7-1 to the Blades! He reappeared later in the season but couldn't prevent the club from being relegated to the second division. Winning a regular place the following season, he was the club's first-choice keeper in 1904/05 when Bolton regained their top-flight status as runners-up to Liverpool. During the course of the 1931/32 season, the Wanderers signed Jimmy Boyle from the Bear Park club in Durham but he too didn't have the best of debuts, playing his first game in a 7-1 defeat at Sheffield Wednesday – a game in which Harold Blackmore gave Bolton an early lead! Another player who had a debut to forget was former Manchester City and England wing-half Mike Doyle. Signed from Stoke City as the Whites attempted to bolster their defence, he put through his own goal in a 1-1 draw at Oldham Athletic. Worse was to come as he was sent off in his next game at Newcastle United.

FA CUP FINAL 1953

Nationwide sympathy was in favour of Bolton's opponents, Blackpool, and especially Stanley Matthews who was looking for the Cup winners' medal that had eluded him in both the 1948 and 1951 finals. The Wanderers broke away to open the scoring after only 75 seconds. Doug Holden, on the right, found Lofthouse in front of goal and he scored with a snap-shot from 28 yards which George Farm in the Blackpool goal failed to gather when he seemed to have the ball covered. Blackpool drew level in the 37th minute when Harold Hassall deflected a Stan Mortensen shot that appeared to be going wide. The Wanderers, though, were soon ahead when Willie Moir beat Farm after good work by Holden and Bobby Langton on the Bolton right. Eric Bell, the Bolton right-back, had been injured and caused a re-shuffle of the Wanderers team, yet it was he who headed his team into a 3-1 lead. With 66 minutes of the game gone, Matthews crossed and Stan Hanson in the Bolton goal failed to hold the ball as it dropped and Mortensen was too quick for the keeper, pushing the ball just inside the post. The equaliser came when Mortensen took a free-kick from outside the penalty area, hammering the ball home with Hanson unsighted. With several Bolton players limping, there was no stopping Matthews and he dribbled his way along to finish with a pass to Bill Perry, who crashed his shot into the net from a few yards out. The Wanderers had collapsed in one of the most exciting FA Cup Finals in history and Stanley Matthews had his FA Cup winners' medal. Bolton's route to the final was as follows:

Round	Opposition	Score
Third	Fulham (h)	3-1
Holden, Moir, Lofthouse		
Fourth	Notts County (h)	1-1
Lofthouse		
Fourth (replay)	Notts County (a)	2-2
Moir 2		
Fourth (2nd replay)	Notts County (n)*	1-0
Lofthouse		
Fifth	Luton Town (a)	1-0
Lofthouse		
Sixth	Gateshead (a)	1-0
Lofthouse		
Semi-final	Everton(n)**	4-3
Moir, Lofthouse 2, Holden		
Final	Blackpool (n)***	3-4
Lofthouse, Moir, Bell		

played at Hillsborough, Sheffield
**played at Maine Road, Manchester*
***played at Wembley Stadium*

Bolton's 1953 FA Cup Final team:Hanson, Ball, R Banks, Wheeler, Barrass, Bell, Holden, Moir, Lofthouse, Hassall, Langton.

BARGAIN BUY

After beginning his Football League career with Preston North End, winger Peter Thompson joined Liverpool for £35,000 in August 1963. There were few more exciting sights in the game than Thompson running at defenders with the ball at his feet. In nine seasons at Anfield he played in just over 400 games, scoring 54 goals. In his first season with the Reds he won four England Under-23 caps and also played his first full international. He was eventually capped 16 times for England while at Anfield, collecting League and FA Cup honours as well. After losing his place to Steve Heighway he joined Bolton on loan in December 1973 and made his debut in a 1-0 home win over Sunderland. A month later he signed on a permanent basis for a fee of just £18,000, giving the Wanderers an exciting new attacking dimension. A great crowd favourite, he helped the club through one of its most exciting periods but at the end of the 1977/78 season, in which he had played in 132 matches, he left the game to run a hotel in the Lake District.

THIRD TIME LUCKY

After failing at the play-off stages in successive seasons, the Wanderers finally made it in 2000/01, securing a place at football's top table for the third time in the space of seven seasons. When chairman Phil Gartside and Big Sam teamed up in October 1999, neither could have imagined promotion to the Premiership so soon. Forced to sell some of his prized possessions – Mark Fish, Eidur Gudjohnsen and Claus Jensen – Allardyce had to beg and borrow players to rebuild his squad under the most severe of financial restraints but even so, he brought the good times rolling back. Having beaten West Bromwich Albion in the two-legged semi-final, Bolton faced local rivals Preston North End at the Millennium Stadium in Cardiff. Gareth Farrelly opened the scoring in the 16th minute and then, after the introduction of Michael Ricketts, it was Farrelly who sent the substitute away for his 24th goal of the season. Ricardo Gardner applied the finishing touch with what was almost the last kick of the game to give the Wanderers a 3-0 win. Was it a lucky win? The Wanderers were assigned the lucky dressing-room, the fans were at the lucky end of the stadium and in Michael Ricketts – 13 of his 23 goals came from the bench – they had their lucky charm!

FIRST OVERSEAS TOUR

After winning the second division championship in 1908/09, Bolton Wanderers embarked on their first-ever overseas tour to Holland. They won all five games played on the continent, scoring 31 goals and conceding just three. The results were: HBS Hague (4-1), Sparta Rotterdam (3-0), Swallows FC (6-0), AFS (8-1) and Dordrecht (10-1).

MOST INTERNATIONAL CAPS

England	Nat Lofthouse	1950-1958	33
Scotland	John McGinlay	1994-1997	14
Wales	Ted Vizard	1911-1926	22
Northern Ireland	Gerry Taggart	1996-1998	10
Republic of Ireland	Jason McAteer	1994-1995	14

OFF TO A FLYER

There's always a special buzz when the Wanderers are at home on the opening day of the season. New players on the pitch, fans sporting the latest replica kit off it and just occasionally a different face in the home dug-out – it all adds up to a tremendously exciting mix of the familiar and the unknown. For Bolton fans everywhere, of course, there's no better way to start the season than with a thumping win, whether at home or on the road. Here are ten memorable opening day victories, stretching back to the early years of the club.

Year	Result	Final League Position
1893	Bolton 4 Stoke City 1	10th in the First Division
1926	Leeds United 2 Bolton 5	4th in the First Division
1934	Charlton Athletic 1 Bolton 4	2nd in the Second Division
1949	Bolton 4 Stoke City 0	16th in the First Division
1951	Bolton 5 Aston Villa 2	5th in the First Division
1956	Bolton 4 Blackpool 1	9th in the First Division
1958	Bolton 4 Leeds United 0	4th in the First Division
1969	Bolton 4 Millwall 1	16th in the Second Division
1970	Bolton 4 Luton Town 2	22nd in the Second Division
2001	Leicester City 0 Bolton 5	16th in the Premiership

THE BURNDEN DISASTER

It was on the afternoon of 9 March 1946 that Burnden Park became the scene of one of the worst disasters the English game has known, yet though 33 people were killed, many people present at the game were unaware of the tragedy. An estimated 85,000 crowd had poured into Burnden Park – the official 'gate' figure was only 65,410 – for the second leg of an FA Cup sixth-round tie against Stoke City. The crowd was so tightly packed that many spectators tried to get out of the ground. As the pressure mounted, two crash barriers collapsed. Spectators were hurtled forward and many were trampled underfoot. Dead and wounded were laid out on the running track, doctors being summoned from the crowd to attend to them. The game was just 12 minutes old when the referee was informed of the full extent of the disaster. He took the players off the field but after consultation with the police, play was resumed after a 12-minute break. It was felt that this was the wisest decision. Play continued until its finish with no interval being taken. In addition to the 33 fatalities, 500 were injured, 24 of whom were taken to hospital. The Mayor of Bolton opened a Relief Fund and a total of almost £40,000 was raised. The match itself ended in a goalless draw, so Bolton, having won the first leg 2-0, went through to the semi-finals where they lost to Charlton Athletic.

HOME GOAL AVALANCHE

Bolton's final three home games of the 1894/95 season, their last at the Pikes Lane ground, saw them score 13 goals. Wins of 4-3 against Nottingham Forest and 4-1 against Aston Villa were followed by a 5-0 thrashing of West Bromwich Albion. Albion were handicapped as their keeper James Reader was sent off for pushing Willie Joyce. The Wanderers hammered home their advantage with Peter Turnbull, who had joined Bolton from Burnley a month earlier, netting a second-half hat-trick. The result ensured Bolton's safety from the end-of-season Test Matches and although the final game of the campaign was lost 5-0 at Sheffield United, the club's home form of seven wins and a draw in their last eight outings at Pikes Lane pulled them through from an almost hopeless position.

TRADEGY: THE BURNDEN DISASTER

LEAGUE CUP MARATHON

After victories over Rochdale and Watford – each over two legs –in the 1989/90 Littlewoods Cup, the Wanderers were drawn away at Swindon Town in what proved to be a marathon tie. After twice leading, the Whites found themselves 3-2 down with just a couple of minutes remaining. Substitute Mark Came struck an equaliser to take the clubs back to Burnden Park a week later. Following a 1-1 draw, the clubs tossed up for choice of venue for the third meeting but with Bolton again having home advantage they could only draw, with Tony Philliskirk netting from the penalty spot. The tie was finally settled after a marathon seven and a half hours of football, when the Robins scored deep into injury time in the fourth meeting at the County Ground against a Wanderers side weakened by injury!

UNBEATABLE NAT

Wanderers' legendary centre-forward Nat Lofthouse three times played in goal against Wolves, without conceding and even saved a penalty! The first time he had to don the No.1 jersey was on 11 February 1956. Bolton's debutant keeper, 16-year-old Joe Dean had to go off for stitches to a cut just above his eye. Though he was only between the posts for ten minutes or so, he produced a wonderful save to keep out a Ron Flowers' header. With Dean back in goal, Lofthouse went back up front and equalised almost immediately although Wolves went on to win 4-2. Again at Molineux about a year later, Nat had an even longer spell in goal. The game played on 2 February 1957, saw Wolves leading 3-0 when Eddie Hopkinson broke a finger. Not only did Lofty's saves inspire 10-men Wanderers to pull the game back to 3-2 but the deputy keeper even saved a Harry Hooper penalty in the dying minutes! In the FA Charity Shield at Burnden Park on 5 October 1958, Dean dislocated his shoulder and again Lofthouse went in goal before Hopkinson, who had been watching the game from the Manchester Road stand, was able to get changed and take Dean's place. Again Wolves failed to beat Nat, who was later twice on target in a 4-1 win for Bolton.

PLAYED AND MANAGED

Eight men have played for and managed Bolton Wanderers. Former right-back John Somerville became the club's first secretary-manager and was in charge from 1908 to 1910. Walter Rowley, who had been groomed and influenced by the long-serving Charles Foweraker, took charge from 1944 to 1950. The legendary Nat Lofthouse had two spells in charge, 1968 to 1970 and in 1985. Former Nottingham Forest midfielder John McGovern was the club's player-manager from 1982 to 1985 and he was followed by popular goalkeeper Charlie Wright, also in 1985. At the end of that year former Liverpool and England full-back Phil Neal took over the reins – he was the club's boss until 1992. Sam Allardyce, of course, had a couple of spells as a player before managing the club from 1999 to 2007. He was replaced by former Liverpool midfielder Sammy Lee, who had appeared in four games for the club.

BEST DEFENDER?

The best footballing centre-half to have played for the Wanderers since the Second World War – and possibly the best English defender never bestowed with international honours – Paul Jones joined the club on leaving school in Ellesmere Port. After progressing through the club's junior ranks, he was one of a number of teenagers who played against Sheffield United in January 1971, a match the Wanderers won 2-1. After replacing John Hulme at the start of the following season, Jones missed very few games over the next 12 seasons and was ever-present in 1972/73, 1974/75 and 1976/77. He won a third division championship medal in 1973 and five years later a second division championship medal, though he sustained an injury that restricted his appearances during that campaign. During the club's stay in the first division he had a spell at right-back but lacked the pace to fill the role on a regular basis. Following the club's relegation to the third division, Jones, who had scored 43 goals in 506 games, left the Wanderers to play for Huddersfield Town. After that he was called up into the England squad during Don Revie's reign as manager and had spells with Oldham Athletic and Blackpool before playing non-league football for a number of clubs.

ALLITERATIVE BOLTON XI

A team comprised of former and current Bolton players with the same first and second initials.

<pre>
Jussi Jaaskelainen 1998-
Brian Borrows 1982-1984
Harry Hubbick 1936-1946
Charlie Cooper 1960-1968
Jimmy Jones 1920-1922
Scott Sellars 1995-1997
Brian Birch 1954-1963
George Gibson 1927-1933
Walter White 1903-1909
Harold Hassall 1951-1954
Stuart Storer 1987-1992
Marshall McEwan 1905-1910
</pre>

MONTGOMERY OF ALAMEIN

In November 1949, Field Marshall Viscount Montgomery came to Bolton to be created the 10th – and at that time the only living – Freeman of Bolton. Later that day he went on to Burnden Park, where he met the Wanderers players and their opponents that day, Newcastle United. Unfortunately, he had to leave at half-time but later wrote a letter to the chairman, saying how pleased he was to have met the team and thought that at up to the point of his departure, they were the better side. Final score: Bolton 2 Newcastle 2.

CUP DEFEAT, BUT WANDERERS PROGRESS!

Strange as it may seem, the Wanderers went through to the next round of the FA Cup after losing their previous game. How come? Well, in the 1945/46 season, FA Cup ties were played over two legs and after beating Liverpool 5-0 at Burnden Park, Bolton lost 2-0 at Anfield in the second leg but still went into the draw for the fifth round. They eventually lost 2-0 to Charlton Athletic at Villa Park in the semi-final.

FIRST THINGS FIRST

As managers often like to point out, it's always nice to get off to a good start and generally speaking, the Wanderers have done pretty well when they've found themselves in a new competition – as you can see from these results in a variety of leagues and cups.

Year	Competition	Result
1881	FA Cup	Bolton 5 Eagley 5
1888	Football League	Bolton 3 Derby County 6
1958	FA Charity Shield	Bolton 4 Wolves 1
1960	League Cup	Hull City 0 Bolton 1
1976	Anglo-Scottish	Bolton 0 Blackpool 0
1983	Associate Members Cup	Burnley 2 Bolton 1
1993	Anglo-Italian Cup	Tranmere Rovers 1 Bolton 2
2005	UEFA Cup	Bolton 2 Lokomotiv Plovdiv 1

FA CUP HAT-TRICK HEROES

Thirteen players have scored FA Cup hat-tricks for Bolton, the last being Dean Holdsworth against Scunthorpe United back in 2001.

Player	Season	Opponents
Billy Struthers	1882/83	Bootle (h)
Billy Struthers	1883/84	Bolton Olympic (h)
James Turner	1888/89	West Manchester (h)
David Weir	1889/90	Belfast Distillery (h)
James Cassidy	1889/90	Sheffield United (h)
David Weir	1889/90	Sheffield United (h)
James Brogan	1889/90	Sheffield United (h)
Sam Marsh	1907/08	Everton (h)
Joe Smith	1913/14	Swindon Town (h)
John Reid Smith	1926/27	Blackpool (a)
Jack Milsom	1933/34	Brighton & Hove Albion (h)
Ray Westwood	1945/46	Liverpool (h)
Roy Greaves	1971/72	Rossendale United (a)
John Byrom	1973/74	Stoke City (h)
Dean Holdsworth	2000/01	Scunthorpe United (h)

WALKWAY OF FAME

Bolton Wanderers are well known for being a family club, constantly looking for opportunities to offer support and care to the club's supporters. In 2002, the Walkway of Fame was inaugurated to celebrate 125 years and is now an ongoing feature situated outside the Main Reception. It presents an opportunity for Bolton fans to celebrate special events by having a message inscribed on a brick and laid within the Walkway – alongside the club's very own 'Stars of Past and Present'. Such names as Nat Lofthouse, Sam Allardyce, Eddie Hopkinson, Peter Reid, Frank Worthington and Gudni Bergsson and many, many more all feature.

BOLTON'S TOP GOALSCORERS

Competition	Player	Goals
Football League	Nat Lofthouse	255
FA Cup	Nat Lofthouse	27
League Cup	John McGinlay	14
Associate Members Cup	Tony Caldwell	10

A BAD KNIGHT FOR THE WANDERERS

Having drawn the first leg of the 1999/2000 first division play-off semi-final at the Reebok 2-2 with Ipswich Town, Bolton travelled to Portman Road for the return. The game was refereed by Kent official Barry Knight, who turned a pulsating match into complete and utter chaos. He awarded three penalties and an unbelievable 12 yellow and two red cards to Bolton players, yet didn't see fit to caution a single home player! There was less than a minute of normal time remaining when Northern Ireland international and current Town boss Jim Magilton rescued Ipswich with a dramatic equaliser to take the game into extra time. Then Big Sam saw his side go down to nine men as Robbie Elliott followed Mike Whitlow to the dressing-room. Ipswich went on to win 5-3 with Allardyce wishing the victors well before unleashing a most fierce verbal assault on Mr Knight which, even by his own tough-talking standards, was ferocious.

ON THE WALKWAY OF FAME: PETER REID

WANDERERS LOSE TO CHORLEY!

One of the biggest-ever upsets to occur at Burnden Park was when non-league club Chorley beat the Wanderers – but not Bolton, it was fourth division Wolverhampton Wanderers. Chorley had been drawn at home to face the once mighty Wolves but their Victory Park ground was unable to hold the anticipated attendance and so the game was switched to Burnden Park. A 1-1 draw resulted and with the same scoreline in the replay at Molineux, the second replay came back to Burnden. A crowd of 5,421 saw the Magpies embarrass Wolves by winning 3-0.

EVER-PRESENTS

The first Bolton Wanderers players to have 100% appearance records for the club in a season's League matches were James Brogan, Kenny Davenport and John Milne, who all played in the 22 games of the inaugural season of the Football League in 1888/89. There have been 68 Bolton players who have been ever-present throughout a Football League season. The greatest number of ever-present seasons by a Wanderers' player is five, the record being held by Eddie Hopkinson and Alex Paton. Bolton's current keeper Jussi Jaaskelainen had been ever-present in four seasons and had not missed a game in the 2007/08 season until he was injured in March.

THE SHERPA VAN TROPHY 1989

Three years after losing 3-0 to Bristol City in the Freight Rover Trophy final, Bolton were back at Wembley in the same competition, although by now it was called the Sherpa Van Trophy. In 1988/89, the Wanderers at times played so well that it seemed their name was on the trophy all along. Between Steve Thompson setting the ball rolling with his last-minute penalty in the first qualifying match and clinching a Wembley place – again from the penalty spot – at Blackpool, Wanderers led a charmed life. It was Mark Winstanley with his 40-yard spectacular shot who turned Wanderers' season on its head as they came back from 1-0 down against Wrexham to win 3-1. Phil Brown did a similar salvage job at Crewe in the Northern Area semi-final, whilst Blackpool midfielder Russell Coughlin will always be remembered for the miss that turned the Northern Final in Wanderers' favour. When he almost hit the 'Normid' sign on the Co-op wall from the penalty spot, you got the impression that Bolton were on their way. Wanderers' opponents at Wembley were Torquay United and it was the Devon club that took the lead through Dean Edwards after 23 minutes. Julian Darby equalised five minutes later and Jeff Chandler netted a second, his shot wrong-footing the Torquay keeper after it was deflected by defender John Morrison. Dave Felgate made two excellent saves as United went in search of an equaliser but this meant that they left huge gaps at the back. First Chandler raced forward and found the unmarked Dean Crombie, who netted his first-ever Bolton goal, and three minutes later substitute Stuart Storer crossed for Trevor Morgan to hit a fourth. When the team returned to the town, thousands of ecstatic Bolton fans crowded the streets with a glorious homecoming their Wembley heroes will never forget.

Round	Opposition	Score
Group	Preston North End (h)	1-0

Thompson (pen)

Group	Bury (a)	0-1
First	Preston North End (a)	1-0

Darby

Second	Wrexham (h)	3-1

Winstanley 2, Savage

Semi-final	Crewe Alexandra (a)	2-1

Winstanley, Brown

Area Final 1	Blackpool (h)	1-0

Darby

Area Final 2	Blackpool (a)	1-1

Thompson (pen)

Final	Torquay United (n)*	4-1

Darby, Morrison (og), Crombie, Morgan

* played at Wembley Stadium

Bolton's team in the 1989 Sherpa Van Trophy final was: Felgate, Brown, Cowdrill, Savage, Crombie, Winstanley, Chandler (Storer), Thompson, Thomas, Morgan, Darby.

CRICKETING TROTTERS

There are two Bolton Wanderers players who were also cricketers of real note. Harry Smith played first-class cricket for Gloucestershire and appeared in one Test for England against the West Indies in 1928. A career total of 13,330 runs shows evidence of his reliability as a batsman and 705 dismissals – 441 caught and 264 stumped – from 393 matches puts him way up in a class of his own among Gloucestershire wicketkeepers. For the Wanderers he made only eight league appearances, scoring one goal in the 1913/14 season. Australian-born Ken Grieves played in 452 first-class matches for Lancashire from 1949 to 1964, scoring 20,802 runs at 33.39 and capturing 235 wickets at 28.80. He kept goal for the Wanderers, making 50 first-team appearances.

FINAL WOES

Considering Bolton's illustrious history, the six defeats the Whites have suffered in major finals is not a bad return. Apologies to those who were keen to forget these occasions, but here they are anyway!

Date	Competition	Opponents	Score
31 Mar 1894	FA Cup	Notts County	1-4
23 Apr 1904	FA Cup	Manchester City	0-1
2 May 1953	FA Cup	Blackpool	3-4
24 May 1986	FR Trophy	Bristol City	0-3
2 Apr 1995	League Cup	Liverpool	1-2
29 Feb 2004	League Cup	Middlesbrough	1-2

YOUNG GUN, OLD STAGER

The youngest player to appear for Bolton is Ray Parry, who made his Wanderers debut at the age of 15 years 267 days against Wolverhampton Wanderers at Molineux on 13 October 1951 in a match the Whites lost 5-1. The oldest player to have pulled on a Wanderers shirt is legendary goalkeeper Peter Shilton, who was aged 45 years 239 days when he also played against Wolverhampton Wanderers in the play-off semi-final first leg at Molineux on 14 May 1995, a match Bolton lost 2-1 before winning the return 2-0.

LOCAL BOY MAKES GOOD

One of the greatest of all Wanderers wingers, Billy Butler began his career with his local club Atherton, for whom he signed after being demobbed from the Army. The Wanderers spotted him playing for Atherton in the Bolton Combination and brought him to Burnden Park in April 1920, converting him from centre-forward to outside-right. After making his debut in a 2-0 home defeat at the hands of Chelsea, Butler became a virtual ever-present in the Wanderers' side for the next 12 seasons. He won an England cap against Scotland in 1924, partnering David Jack, and also claimed three FA Cup winners' medals in the 1920s, scoring the opening goal in the 1929 final, when Bolton beat Portsmouth 2-0. After the Wanderers were relegated in 1933, Butler asked to go on the transfer list and having scored 74 goals in 449 League and Cup games, left Burnden Park to join his former team-mate Joe Smith, who was manager of Reading. When Smith left to join Blackpool, Butler replaced him as manager of Reading but resigned four years later for personal reasons. He later managed Torquay United before emigrating to South Africa where he coached and managed a number of clubs.

EX-FILES

A team of former Whites now playing elsewhere in English football.

1 Matt Glennon...........Huddersfield Town
2 Tel Ben Haim ....Chelsea
3 Robbie Elliott ....Hartlepool United
4 Alan Stubbs .... Derby County
5 Bruno N'Gotty..................Leicester City
6 Radhi Jaidi ....Birmingham City
7 Abdoulaye Faye...........Newcastle United
8 Gary Speed .... Sheffield United
9 Nicolas Anelka............................Chelsea
10 Adranik Teymourian.................Fulham
11 Henrik Pedersen ....Hull City

Manager: Phil Brown..................Hull City

UEFA CUP 2005-06

Having qualified for the Uefa Cup for the first time in the club's history, the Wanderers were drawn to face Bulgarian side Lokomotiv Plovdiv in the first round of the competition. In the first leg at the Reebok, the visitors took the lead against the run of play but Wanderers levelled when El Hadji Diouf headed home Nicky Hunt's cross. Mexican international Jared Borgetti made sure Bolton's first European game ended in triumph when he netted an injury-time winner from a tight angle. In the return leg, the Bulgarians opened the scoring to level the scores on aggregate but an Alexsandar Tunchev own goal and a late strike from skipper Kevin Nolan saw off Plovdiv's challenge. Bolton were handed a difficult draw for the group stage being paired with Besiktas, Sevilla, FC Zenit and Vitoria Guimaraes. With three teams qualifying from the group, Bolton were hopeful, especially after a Borgetti goal had helped them to a 1-1 draw against group favourites Besiktas in Turkey. A Nolan goal gave the Wanderers a 1-0 success over Zenit whilst a late Ricardo Vaz Te strike levelled the scores against Vitoria Guimaraes. Bolton's last group game against Sevilla also ended in a 1-1 draw with Bruno N'Gotty netting for the Wanderers.

Final Group Table

	P	W	D	L	F	A	Pts
Sevilla	4	2	1	1	8	4	7
Zenit St Petersburg	4	2	1	1	5	4	7
BOLTON WANDERERS	4	1	3	0	4	3	6
Besiktas	4	1	2	1	5	6	5
Vitoria Guimaraes	4	0	1	3	4	9	1

In the knockout stages, Bolton were drawn to face highly fancied French outfit Marseille. The first leg at the Reebok was goalless and though Stelios gave the Whites the lead in France, Marseille drew level through Franck Ribery before knocking Bolton out of the competition after Tal Ben Haim put through his own goal.

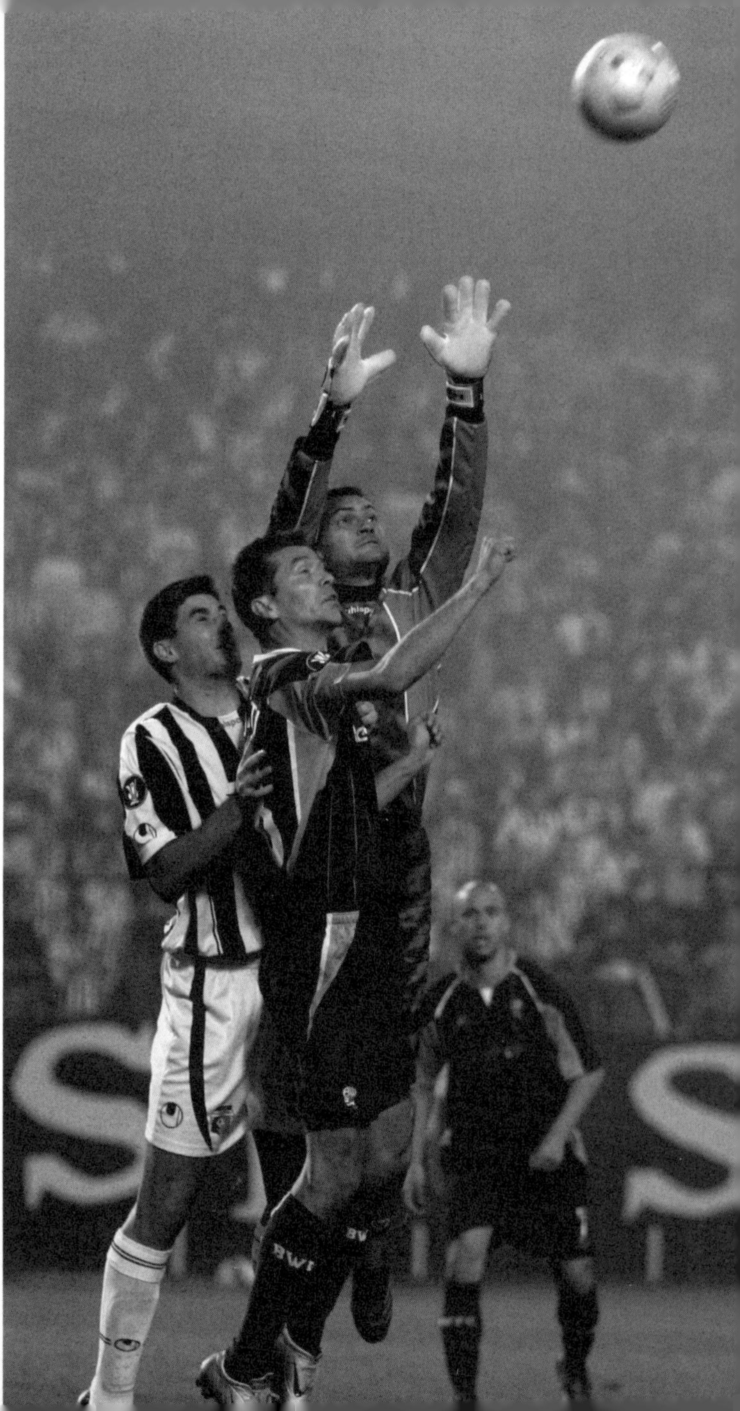

WANDERERS IN UEFA CUP ACTION AGAINST LOKOMOTIV PLOVDIV

THE OVAL-BALL GAME

Burnden Park and the Reebok have hosted a number of rugby league finals and international games. The first game was on 23 January 1985 when the Swinton Lions faced the Sheffield Eagles. The game was played at Burnden because the pitch was frost-free due to undersoil heating. The game began 20 minutes late after Sheffield's coach broke down coming over the Pennines. An untimely blizzard kept the Wednesday night attendance to 1,438, half the anticipated figure but close to Swinton's average for the season. Swinton won 14-8 on a pitch that played well despite the fact that on the previous evening the Wanderers had beaten Crewe Alexandra in the Freight Rover Trophy; three days later Rotherham United were beaten 2-0 in a League game.

PACK OF THREE

Hat-trick pioneers for the club:

First in the FA Cup
Billy Struthers v Bootle (home 6-0) .... on 4 November 1882

First in the first division
David Weir v Accrington (home 4-1) ....on 22 December 1888

First in the second division
Jimmy Hanson v Barnsley (away 6-1) ....on 26 December 1899

First in League Cup
Nat Lofthouse v Grimsby Town (home 6-2)...on 26 October 1960

First in the third division
Stuart Lee v Halifax Town (home 3-0) ....on 16 April 1973

First in the fourth division
John Thomas v Peterborough United (away 4-0)...30 January 1988

First in the Associate Members Cup
David Reeves v Rochdale (home 4-1) ....on 10 December 1991

WONDERFUL WESTWOOD!

Ray Westwood played his early football with Stourbridge and Brierley Hill Alliance before having a trial with Aston Villa. Fortunately for the Wanderers this came to nothing and on the recommendation of former centre-half Jack Round, they secured his services on amateur forms in the summer of 1928. He turned professional in March 1931 and made his first team debut in a 1-1 home draw against Manchester City. Forming a formidable partnership with Willie Cook, Westwood's performances led to him representing the Football League and winning six full caps for England, the first against Wales in September 1934. In 1934/35, when the Wanderers finished runners-up to Brentford in the second division and so won promotion to the top flight, Westwood scored 30 goals in 38 League games, including four in the 8-0 home win over Barnsley, all of his goals coming in the first 39 minutes of the match. During the 1937/38 season, when the Wanderers finished seventh in the first division, Westwood was the club's top scorer with 23 goals in 33 League games, including hat-tricks against Chelsea (home 5-5) and Grimsby Town (home 3-1). He continued to play for the Wanderers after the Second World War, taking his tally of goals to 144 in 333 League and Cup games before joining Chester. After ending his career with Darwen, he returned to his home-town Brierley Hill and became a newsagent.

RECORD LEAGUE WIN

Bolton's 8-0 victory over Barnsley on 6 October 1934 included an incredible spell of five goals in the final six minutes of the second division match. Bolton took the lead after 21 minutes through Ray Westwood, who went on to complete a first-half hat-trick with further goals in the 33rd and 39th minutes. Wanderers continued to dominate after the break but it wasn't until the 84th minute that the floodgates finally began to open. GT Taylor netted twice inside a minute before Bob Shotton put through his own goal. To add to a sensational climax, Westwood netted his fourth with a fine solo effort and, in the last minute, Jack Milsom made it 8-0. The Burnden crowd rose to the players as they left the field, the result taking them to the top of the table.

BURNDEN PARK

Bolton's new site following their departure from Pikes Lane was a former chemical works, bordered by a railway embankment and viaduct over the River Croal and a line of cottages along Manchester Road. A Scarborough contractor was called in to lay out the new ground under instructions from John Norris, one of the club's directors, who specifically requested a cycling track round the pitch, just like the one laid for the King of Italy! Burnden Park opened on 17 August 1895 with an athletics meeting, the town's ninth Annual Athletics Festival, attended by an impressive crowd of almost 20,000. Between events the enthusiastic audience were treated to a high-diver, a performer on stilts and a monkey on a bicycle! On Wednesday 11 September 1895 the ground was eventually put to its proper use when Preston North End were the visitors for a benefit game for Di Jones. The crowd of 3,000 saw North End win the game with a solitary goal from David Smith. Three days later the first League game took place at Burnden Park with Everton as the visitors. The game was preceded by a cycle race an hour before the kick-off, witnessed by a 10,000 crowd which grew to 15,000 by 4 pm – the advertised start – and Bolton won the game 3-1. However, over the next few weeks the pitch, which had been laid upon barrels of cotton bales, became such a quagmire that the reserves had to play one of their games at Pikes Lane and in one match, Preston refused to come out for the second half after a sudden downpour had flooded the playing area. To cure this problem, the drainage was improved by increasing the pitch's camber in 1896. It wasn't too long before Burnden Park began to attract some important games and in April 1901 it was chosen as the venue for the FA Cup Final replay between Sheffield United and Tottenham Hotspur. The club's run to the 1904 FA Cup Final helped finance the building of the Main Stand at a cost of £3,500. A year later the club won promotion to the first division and after having their lease extended by ten years, also had the cycle track removed to make room for the now much larger attendances. In 1906 the Great Lever End was terraced and covered and after the club had purchased the freehold on the ground in 1914, a wing was added to the Main Stand. After the club's second FA Cup win in the 1920s, the old Darcy Lever Stand was replaced by the new Burnden Stand seating 2,750. Burnden Park's official highest crowd was 69,912 for the visit of Manchester City in the FA Cup in February 1933. During the Second World War the ground was taken over, the pitch for use by the Education Authority and the stands by the Ministry of Supply. The Burnden Stand was still full of food supplies when the event which was to stand out in the history of all football grounds occurred on 9 March 1946, during the cup-tie against Stoke. As the game began hundreds spilled out on to the track but it was not until 12 minutes later that it became apparent that there had been fatalities – 33 bodies were found and laid out on the pitch while first aid was given to many more. After the Government report in 1947 the club spent £5,500 modernising the Railway End, improving the turnstiles and gates, adding barriers and fencing off the railway line. On 14 October 1957 Bolton's new floodlights were switched on for a friendly against Hearts. Despite the club's fall from the top flight during the 1960s, Burnden hosted two FA Cup semi-finals. The post-war crowd record at Burnden came in February 1959 when 58,692 were at a fifth round FA Cup tie against Preston North End and even as recently as 1977, the ground housed 50,413 for the League Cup semi-final second leg against Everton. During the summer of 1979, 4,342 seats were put on the Great Lever End and the pitch, a poor drainer despite its camber, was dug up. All manner of compressed rotting matter was found underneath. Undersoil heating and sprinklers were installed, though at one stage it seemed inevitable that a plastic pitch would be laid. This was vetoed by the Football League ruling that banned all further pitches of that nature for three years. The greatest change took place in 1986 when the 16,000 Railway End terrace was cut in half by a Normid Superstore built in the north-west corner of the Embankment on the very spot that had seen the disaster. After the Taylor Report reduced Burnden's capacity to 22,616 in 1995, the club decided to cut its losses at Burnden and relocate to a new site in Lostock. Thus Bolton's last game at Burnden Park was on 25 April 1997 when they beat Charlton Athletic 4-1.

TWO TIME TROTTERS

Players who enjoyed two or more separate playing spells on the books of Bolton Wanderers include:

Player	1st Spell	2nd Spell	3rd Spell
Sam Allardyce	1973-1979	1985	
Ian Bailey	1981 (loan)	1984 (loan)	
David Burke	1978-1980	1991-1993	
Jeff Chandler	1981-1984	1987-1989	
David Felgate	1978	1985 (loan)	1986-1991
Per Frandsen	1996-1999	2000-2004	
Jimmy Phillips	1983-1986	1993-2001	
John Thomas	1980-1981	1987-1988	
Neil Whatmore*	1972-1980	1982 (loan)	1983 (loan)

Whatmore had a fourth spell in 1987 but didn't appear in the first team.

LOYAL SERVANT

An England schoolboy and youth international, Warwick Rimmer was a nephew of the former Sheffield Wednesday player Ellis Rimmer and made his debut in the club's first Football League Cup tie at Hull City in October 1960. Strong in the tackle, the Merseyside-born defensive wing-half soon established himself in the Wanderers' side and was ever-present in three seasons. Though he twice suffered relegation with the Trotters, he captained the side that won the third division championship in 1972/73 when his experience helped the young Paul Jones at the heart of the Bolton defence. Rimmer was one of the club's most loyal servants, he played in 528 league and cup games, and scored 17 goals for Bolton – but in March 1975 he left to join Crewe Alexandra. After making 128 league appearances for the Railwaymen he coached and managed the Gresty Road club before coaching moving abroad to coach in Sierra Leone. He returned to England to rejoin Bolton as the club's commercial manager before serving Tranmere Rovers in a similar capacity and later in a coaching role as the youth development officer at Prenton Park.

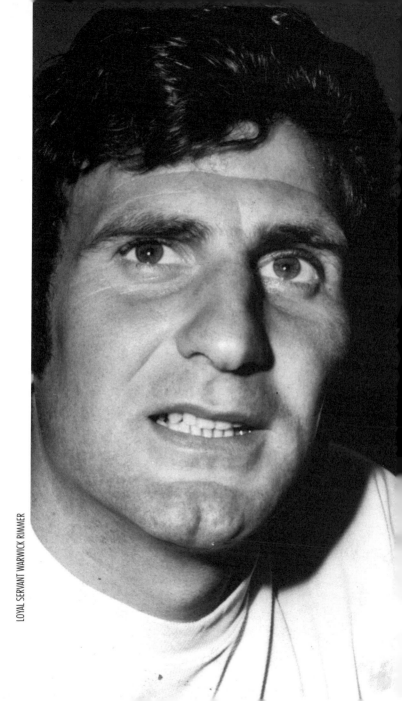

WANDERERS' ANTHEMS

Out of the many football songs and chants heard at Burnden Park and the Reebok, here are a few favourites that have just made it past the censor!

Tune – (Keep) The Red Flag Flying
We'll never die, we'll never die
We'll never die, we'll never die
We'll keep the blue n' white flag flying high
Coz Bolton Wanderers will never die

Tune – You Are My Sunshine
You're just a Scouser
A filthy Scouser
So listen to what I say
Your mum's out thieving
Your dad's drug dealing
So please don't take my hub caps away

Tune – Hey Baby
Heyyyy Kevin Nolan!
Ooh Aah!
I wanna know...
oh–oh–oh (oh–oh–oh) if you'll score a goal

Tune – Winter Wonderland
There's only one John McGinlay
There's only one John McGinlay
Walking Along, Singing a Song
Walking in a McGinlay Wonderland

Tune – Knick-Knack-Paddy-Whack
O-K-O-C-H-A
You've got no-one like Jay Jay
With a Knick-Knack-Paddy-Whack
Give a dog a bone
Why don't you all **** off home!

INTERNATIONAL WHITES

Over the years, Bolton Wanderers have had several internationals. Most of them have been from the home nations and Eire, but there have been plenty of other international caps won by players from all over the world. Denmark and Iceland have the most representatives

Denmark .... Per Frandsen, Claus Jensen
....Henrik Pedersen, Stig Tofting
Finland .... Jussi Jaaskelainen, Mixu Paatelainen, Jani Viander
France...Nicolas Anelka, Youri Djorkaeff
Greece .... Stelios Giannakopoulos, Kostas Konstantinidis
Iceland..................................... Gudni Bergsson, Eider Gudjohnsen
....Arnar Gunnlaugsson Birkir Kristinsson
Iran... Andranik Teymourian
Israel.. Tal Ben Haim, Tamir Cohen
Ivory Coast..Abdoulaye Meite
Jamaica ....Ricardo Gardner, Jermaine Johnson
Japan..................................... Hidetoshi Nakata, Akinori Nishizawa
Mexico.. Jared Borgetti
Nigeria...Blessing Kaku, Jay Jay Okocha
Oman ....Ali Al Habsi
Senegal .... El-Hadji Diouf, Aboulaye Faye, Khalilou Fadiga
Slovakia ....Lubomir Michalik
South Africa...Mark Fish
Tunisia..Radhi Jaidi
Yugoslavia.. Sasa Curcic

SUDDEN DEATH

Bolton's penalty shoot-out results:

Date	Competition	Result	Shoot-Out
14.9.1983	League Cup Rd 1	Chester 2 Bolton 2	lost 0-2
24.8.1993	League Cup Rd 1	Bolton 2 Bury 2	won 3-0
20.12.1995	League Cup Rd 4	Norwich City 0 Bolton 0	lost 2-3
3.10.1998	League Cup Rd 3	Norwich City 1 Bolton 1	won 3-1
2.4.2000	FA Cup semi-final	Aston Villa 0 Bolton 0	lost 1-4
11.9.2001	League Cup Rd 4	Bolton 2 Southampton 2	won 6-5

WERE YOU THERE?

With attendance figures for games at Pikes Lane not available, below are the highest and lowest attendance figures at Burnden Park and the Reebok Stadium for games in various competitions.

Highest League Attendance at Burnden Park
55,477 v Manchester United, First Division, 1 Sep 1951 (won 1-0)

Highest League Attendance at the Reebok
27,880 v Liverpool, Premiership, 29 Aug 2004 (won 1-0)

Highest FA Cup Attendance at Burnden Park
69,912 v Manchester City, fifth round, 18 Feb 1933 (lost 2-4)

Highest FA Cup Attendance at the Reebok
23,523 v Arsenal, sixth round, 12 Mar 2005 (lost 0-1)

Highest League Cup Attendance at Burnden Park
50,413 v Everton, semi-final 2nd leg, 15 Feb 1977 (lost 0-1)

Highest League Cup Attendance at the Reebok
16,302 v Aston Villa, semi-final 1st leg, 20 Jan 2004 (won 5-2)

Highest Associate Members Cup at Burnden Park
12,102 v Wigan Athletic, northern area final, 9 May 1986 (won 2-1)

Highest Uefa Cup Attendance at the Reebok,
26,163 v Atletico Madrid, last 32, 14 Feb 2008, (won 1-0)

Lowest League Attendance at Burnden Park
2,902 v Darlington, Third Division, 5 Nov 1985 (lost 0-3)

Lowest League Attendance at the Reebok
11,668 v Birmingham City, First Division, 5 Sep 1999 (drew 3-3)

Lowest FA Cup Attendance at Burnden Park,
4,652 v Halifax Town, first round, 18 Nov 1896 (drew 1-1)

Lowest FA Cup Attendance at the Reebok
5,734 v Cardiff City, third round, 21 Dec 1999 (won 1-0)

Lowest League Cup Attendance at Burnden Park
2,665 v Chester City, first round, 30 August 1983 (won 3-0)

Lowest League Cup Attendance at the Reebok
3,673 v Gillingham, second round, 21 Sep 1999 (won 2-0)

Lowest Associate Members Cup Attendance at Burnden Park
1,507 v Rochdale, qualifying round, 10 Dec 1991 (won 4-1)

Lowest Uefa Cup Attendance at the Reebok
10,229 v Aris Salonika, group match, 29 Nov 2007 (drew 1-1)

CAPTAIN FANTASTIC

Farnworth-born Roy Greaves made his League debut in October 1965, aged 18, in a 1-0 defeat at Leyton Orient. The following Saturday he played at centre-forward for his first home game and scored both Bolton's goals in a 3-2 defeat by Southampton. He then settled into the Wanderers' die at inside-forward, becoming a regular in 1967/68 when he topped the club's goalscoring charts, as he did the following season. Despite these achievements, he failed to win over the home fans and was often subjected to mindless criticism. The turning point in his career came when manager Jimmy Armfield moved him into midfield after relegation to the third division in 1971. When the Wanderers won the championship in 1972/73, Greaves was ever-present and a cornerstone of the side that spent the next five seasons in the second division before winning a place in the top flight. By then Greaves had become captain and it was he who lifted the second division championship trophy aloft at the end of he 1977/78 season. In his debut season in the first division he missed only one game but the following term a combination of injuries and advancing years cost him his place. He had scored 85 goals in 575 games when in March 1980 he left Bolton to play for the Seattle Sounders in the NASL. After his stint in America he returned to become player-coach at Rochdale, thus giving him the distinction of having played in every division of the League.

BIG SAM

A product of the club's youth side, Sam Allardyce made his League debut for the Wanderers as a teenager against Notts County in November 1973. Following the departure of Don McAllister to Spurs, Allardyce won a regular place at the heart of the Bolton defence and went on to serve the club well as player and boss. During his time at Burnden Park, Allardyce scored a number of spectacular goals, perhaps none more so than the fearsome header from 18 yards against second division promotion rivals Sunderland in December 1975. Impressive in the air, he helped the club win the second division championship in 1977/78 but after relegation two seasons later, Allardyce left to join Sunderland for a fee of £150,000. After just one season at Roker Park, he moved to Millwall, followed by brief spells at both Coventry and Huddersfield before he rejoined the Wanderers. Sadly, he was hampered by injuries and after appearing in 231 games in which he scored 24 goals, he joined Preston North End. After helping the Lilywhites win promotion to the third division he became the club's youth coach before breaking into management with Blackpool. He later took charge of Notts County, leading them to the third division championship in 1997/98 before being appointed manager of Bolton Wanderers on his 45th birthday on 19th October 1999. He began his Bolton managerial career with a 2-2 home draw against Crewe Alexandra on the same night Phil Brown was appointed as his assistant. In his first season in charge at the Reebok Stadium, the Wanderers reached the semi-finals of both the FA and League Cups and the first division play-offs. In 2000/01 he took the club back into the Premiership with a 3-0 play-off final win over Preston North End at the Millennium Stadium. With little money to spend, he moulded a team together that has since managed to retain its top-flight status. Under Sam's leadership, Bolton reached the 2004 League Cup final and qualified for the Uefa Cup on two occasions. Towards the end of the 2006/07 season, Allardyce parted company with the Wanderers, later joining Premiership rivals Newcastle United. Unfortunately for Big Sam, things on Tyneside didn't work out for him and midway through the 2007/08 season, he lost his job.

BOLTON WANDERERS 1977/78 - BIG SAM'S IN THE MIDDLE ROW!

THERE'S ONLY ONE EDDIE HOPKINSON

The holder of the club's appearance record with 578 first team outings between 1956 and 1969, Eddie Hopkinson remains the best goalkeeper the Wanderers have ever had. He became a naturalised Lancastrian when his family moved south from Durham to Royton near Oldham. He soon signed as an amateur for Oldham Athletic and was only 16 years of age when he played in three third division (North) games in 1951/52. At the end of the season, the Latics overlooked him to Bolton's lasting satisfaction. He joined the Wanderers in August 1952, signing professional forms the following November. His meteoric rise began in 1956 when Bolton's regular keeper Ken Grieves couldn't be released from his cricketing duties as Lancashire were chasing county championship honours. Eddie got his chance in the senior side against Blackpool, a match the Wanderers won 4-1 and went through a brilliant first season without missing a game. In the summer of 1957 he was awarded the first of six England Under-23 caps on a tour behind the Iron Curtain. In October of that year he made his first full international appearance against Northern Ireland, going on to win 14 caps. In 1958 he kept a clean sheet to win an FA Cup winners' medal as the Wanderers beat Manchester United 2-0 at Wembley. At Norwich City in January 1969 he broke Bolton's long-standing appearance record set by Alex Finney and but for an injury which kept him out of the side for most of the 1958/59 season and another which put him out of action for a ten-match spell in 1963/64, he would have passed Finney's record much earlier. After injury forced his retirement, he became assistant-trainer at Burnden Park before joining Stockport County as assistant-manager. He later rejoined the Wanderers as goalkeeping coach, but eventually left the game to become a representative for a chemical company.

FA CUP FINAL 1958

The 1958 FA Cup Final went into the record books as Nat Lofthouse's match. Right from the opening whistle, Bolton's centre-forward stamped his authority on the game and helped his side defeat United with two goals. United were rebuilding after the Munich disaster, whilst the Wanderers were the £110 team – none of the players costing more than a signing-on fee. The game was only three minutes old when Lofthouse stabbed home a long sweeping ball from left half Bryan Edwards to put Bolton 1-0 ahead. Outside-right Brian Birch had a field day against future Wanderers boss Ian Greaves whilst the Reds' Irish international keeper Harry Gregg had a nervous game. Only Bobby Charlton offered a threat to the Bolton rearguard and in the 54th minute his vicious swirling shot hit a post and bounced into Eddie Hopkinson's hands. Three minutes later, Dennis Stevens tried a sharp, rising shot that Gregg could only push into the air. As he turned and jumped a second time, Lofthouse stormed in and bundled Gregg and the ball over the line and into the net. It was one of the most controversial goals scored in an FA Cup Final and under today's conditions, Lofty would have most certainly have been red-carded! But the referee was right on the spot and gave the goal without hesitation. Bolton's route to the final was as follows:

Round	Opposition	Score
Third	Preston North End (a)	3-0
Stevens, Parry 2		
Fourth	York City (a)	0-0
Fourth replay	York City (h)	3-0
Birch, Allcock 2		
Fifth	Stoke City (h)	3-1
Lofthouse, Stevens, Parry		
Sixth	Wolves (h)	2-1
Stevens, Parry		
Semi-final	Blackburn Rovers (n)*	2-1
Gubbins 2		
Final	Manchester United (n)**	2-0
Lofthouse 2		

played at Maine Road, Manchester
**played at Wembley Stadium*

Bolton's 1958 FA Cup Final team: Hopkinson, Hartle, Banks, Hennin, Higgins, Edwards, Birch, Stevens, Lofthouse, Parry, Holden.

GOALSCORING DEBUTS

From Bolton's first League game at Pikes Lane on 8 September 1888, a number of players have scored on their debut for the club. That first game saw Kenny Davenport (2) and James Brogan net Wanderers' goals in a 6-3 defeat. Since then there have been plenty of examples of new boys introducing themselves to the fans in the best way possible, with a goal. Here are a few of those first-timers:

Player	Date	Opposition	Score
John Reid Smith	25 Nov 1922	Manchester City	2-1
Harold Blackmore	2 Apr 1927	Sheffield Wednesday	3-2
Jack Milsom	15 Feb 1930	Leeds United	4-2
Nat Lofthouse*	31 Aug 1946	Chelsea	3-4
Francis Lee	5 Nov 1960	Manchester City	3-1
Neil Whatmore*	4 Apr 1973	Swansea City	3-2
Frank Worthington	1 Oct 1977	Stoke City	1-1
Tony Philliskirk	19 Aug 1989	Cardiff City	2-0
Andy Walker	11 Jan 1992	Exeter City	2-2
Michael Ricketts	26 Aug 2000	Preston North End	2-0

each scored twice on their debuts.

James Turner remains the only player to have scored a hat-trick on his first-team debut for the club – a 9-0 second round FA Cup tie victory over West Manchester on 10 November 1888. He had been selected for the previous round's match away at Hurst but the Wanderers' opponents scratched from the competition.

LEAGUE CUP FINAL 2004

The Carling Cup Final was never top of Sam Allardyce's priority list but the nearer the Wanderers got to the Millennium Stadium, the greater became the club's commitment to the competition. A 3-1 win over Walsall in which Brazilian international Mario Jardel netted twice, gave the Wanderers another home tie in the third round against Gillingham, who were beaten 2-0. Drawn away to Liverpool in the next round, the Whites won a place in the quarter-finals with a 3-2 win thanks to a last-minute penalty converted by Youri Djorkaeff. The game against

Southampton was goalless after 90 minutes and it took an extra-time Henrik Pedersen goal to seal victory for the Wanderers. A masterly display in the semi-final first leg at the Reebok saw Aston Villa two goals behind in the opening ten minutes. Jay Jay Okocha was on fire as the Wanderers went on to win 5-2. A backs-to-the-wall struggle in the return saw Villa triumph 2-0 with Bolton hanging on as the Midlands club went in search of a third goal. At the Millennium Stadium, where their opponents were Middlesbrough, Bolton found themselves 2-0 down before some of the fans had managed to find their seats. Joseph-Desire Job put Boro 1-0 up before Emerson Thome brought down the goalscorer and referee Mike Riley awarded the Teesside club a penalty. Boudewijn Zenden slipped as he shaped to take the spot kick and as he struck the ball, got a double-hit that wrong-footed Jussi Jaaskelainen, just enough for the ball to strike his leg and rocket into the roof of the net. Kevin Davies pulled a goal back and Youri Djorkaeff had the chance to level the scores before Ugo Ehiogu seemed to handle a Stelios shot in the 89th minute. But in all honesty, it was one of those days in which the players failed to live up to their reputations.

Round	Opposition	Score
Second	Walsall (h)	3-1

Jardel 2, Nolan

| Third | Gillingham (h) | 2-0 |

Giannakopoulos, Pedersen

| Fourth | Liverpool (a) | 3-2 |

Jardel, Okocha, Djorkaeff (pen)

| Fifth | Southampton (h) | 1-0 |

Pedersen

| Semi-final first leg | Aston Villa (h) | 5-2 |

Okocha 2, Nolan, Giannakopoulos, N'Gotty

| Semi-final second leg | Aston Villa (a) | 0-2 |
| Final | Middlesbrough (n)* | 1-2 |

Davies

*played at the Millennium Stadium, Cardiff

Bolton's 2004 League Cup Final team was: Jaaskelainen, Hunt (Giannakopoulos), Charlton, Campo, N'Gotty, Thome, Nolan, (Javi Moreno), Frandsen (Pedersen), Davies, Djorkaeff, Okocha

OH FRANKIE FRANKIE

Frank Worthington was a talented footballer and an extrovert character who became a footballing hero at Burnden Park in what was a relatively short career there. He began his career with Huddersfield Town and after helping them to win the second division title in 1969/70, the chance came for him to join Liverpool. A fee of £150,000 had been agreed but a medical examination revealed that he had high blood pressure; Leicester City seized their chance and a cut-price Worthington moved to Filbert Street for £80,000. His elegant, effective centre-forward play was rewarded with an England call-up and he went on to make eight appearances at full international level – it should have been many more. He had scored 72 goals in 210 games for the Foxes when he joined Bolton on loan as Ian Greaves was searching for that extra quality to lift the Wanderers into the first division after two near misses. He scored on his debut against Stoke City and was signed permanently for £90,000. He soon rediscovered the style which had made him one of the best strikers in the game and in 1977/78 he helped the Wanderers win the second division championship. The following season he proved his class as a target man and a finisher. Although Bolton struggled against relegation, Worthington ended the season with 24 League goals to top the first division goalscoring charts. His televised goal against Ipswich Town won the Goal of the Season competition. He had scored 38 goals in 93 games when he moved on to Birmingham City for £150,000. He later had spells with Leeds United, Sunderland, Southampton, Brighton, Tranmere, Preston and Stockport County. One of the game's most gifted strikers, he made 757 league appearances in a career that saw him approaching his 40th birthday before he left the first-class game.

MATCH OF THE DAY DEBUT

Bolton Wanderers' first appearance on BBC Television's Match of the Day was in the 1966/67 season. On Saturday 18 March 1967, the Wanderers travelled to Coventry City for a second division game. Bobby Gould gave the Sky Blues the lead but Bolton winger Ronnie Phillips levelled the scores and that's how the game finished.

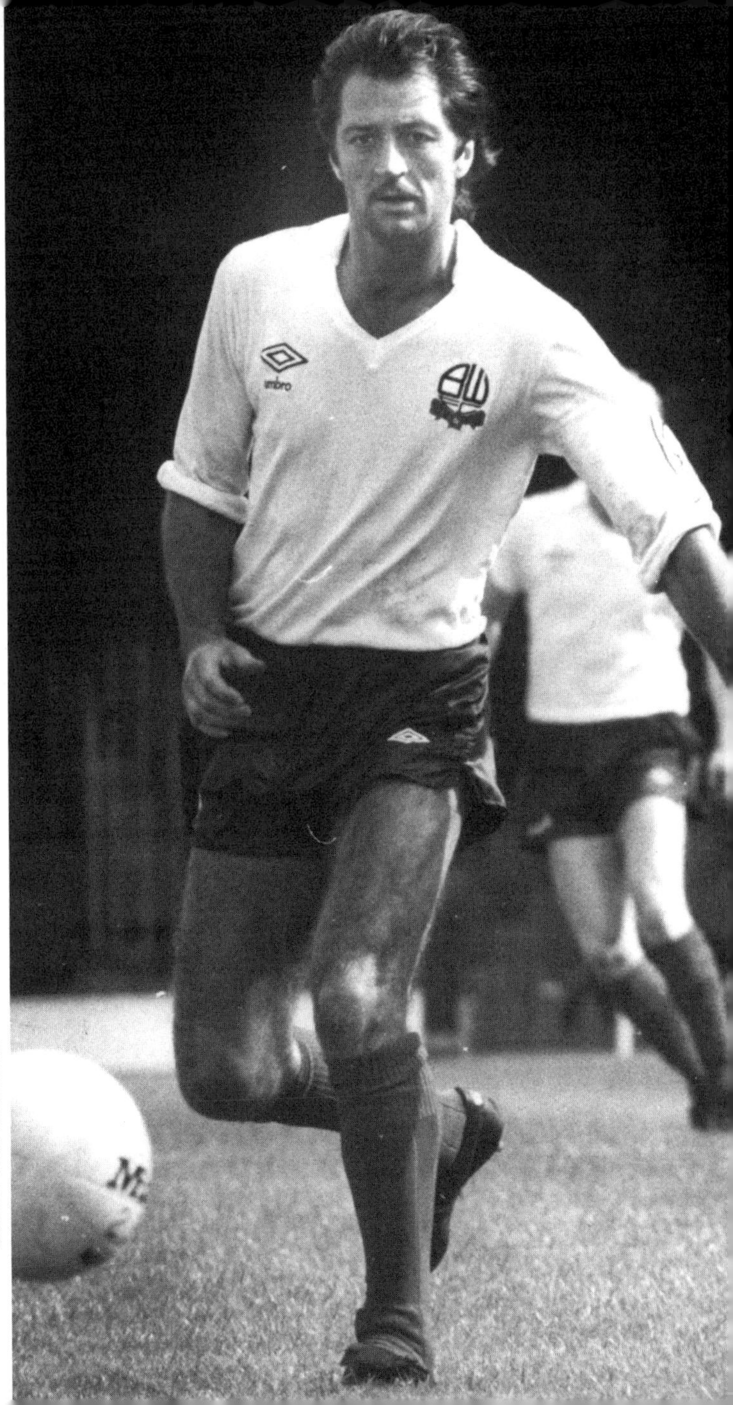

CLASS ACT: FRANK WORTHINGTON

FIRST PROMOTION

Following relegation in 1898/99, Bolton began their first-ever second division campaign the following season. It was new signing Lawrie Bell that had the distinction of scoring the club's first goal in the division in a 3-2 win over Loughborough. Bell then scored twice on his home debut in a 2-1 win over Newton Heath but the club's first reversal came a week later when Sheffield Wednesday (then called The Wednesday) won by the same score. The club's directors offered the team £500 to win promotion and they didn't lose another league game that year. Burnden Park began to buzz when it was realised that the Wanderers had every chance of making an immediate return to the top flight. It was during the Christmas period that Bolton began to take their opponents to task, beating Burton Swifts 5-2, Burnley 6-1 and Loughborough 7-0 in the return. The Wanderers won their next three games before facing Wednesday for a second time. A Bob Jack goal gave them a 1-0 win and extended their lead at the top of the table but the Owls took revenge by knocking Bolton out of the FA Cup. Wanderers' League form then began to suffer before a run of eight wins and a draw in a nine-game spell kept them in the hunt. Promotion was gained with a 3-0 win over Gainsborough Trinity but only 4,327 fans witnessed it! Incredibly, the Wanderers were awarded 11 penalties over the course of the season but all of them were missed! The season was wound up with a 5-0 win over Burton Swifts with Bell, the club's top scorer with 23 goals, netting four times. The win gave Bolton the runners-up spot, two points behind champions The Wednesday. The top of the table looked like this:

	P	W	D	L	F	A	Pts
The Wednesday	34	25	4	5	84	22	54
BOLTON WANDERERS	34	22	8	4	79	25	52
Small Heath	34	20	6	8	78	38	46
Newton Heath	34	20	4	10	63	27	44
Leicester Fosse	34	17	9	8	53	36	43
Grimsby Town	34	17	6	11	67	46	40
Chesterfield	34	16	6	12	65	60	38
Woolwich Arsenal	34	16	4	14	61	43	36
Lincoln City	34	14	8	12	46	43	36

REIDY AND THE BROKEN LEGS

Peter Reid was a member of the successful Huyton Boys side that caused something of an upset when they won the English Schools Trophy in 1970. He had the chance to join a number of clubs as an apprentice but opted for the Wanderers and in October 1974 made his first-team debut as a substitute in a home match against Orient. An ever-present for the next two seasons, Reid's cultured midfield play and his intense desire to be involved at all times were features of Bolton's second division championship-winning side of 1977/78. On New Year's Day 1979 he collided with Everton goalkeeper George Wood on a snow-covered Burnden Park and broke his leg. He eventually returned to the side on a weekly contract but broke his leg again in Bolton's match at Barnsley. He had scored 25 goals in 261 games for the Wanderers when he joined Everton for a bargain price of £60,000 in December 1982. In 1984/85 he was voted the Players' Player of the Year as Everton came close to winning the treble of League, FA Cup and European Cup Winners' Cup. He also represented England at under-21 and senior levels, winning 13 caps and playing at the 1986 World Cup in Mexico under Bobby Robson. After spells as a player-coach, Reid entered management with Manchester City and later Sunderland – where he enjoyed several successes – before taking charge briefly of Leeds United and then at Coventry City.

BOBIC TREBLE SAVES WANDERERS

Bolton Wanderers escaped relegation from the Premiership in 2001-02 after an amazing 4-1 win against Ipswich Town. The Wanderers went ahead after just 71 seconds when German international striker Fredi Bobic picked up a through ball from Kevin Nolan to fire past Marshall. Ipswich were in more trouble when Bobic headed home his and Bolton's second goal after more poor defending. Youri Djorkaeff made it 3-0 and as Ipswich disintegrated at the back, Bobic completed his first-half hat-trick by turning in a Ricardo Gardner corner. Jamie Clapham netted a second-half consolation for the Tractor Boys as Bolton took their foot off the pedal.

THAT'S JUST GREEDY

On 23 occasions, Bolton players have gone on to score more than three goals in one match.

Player	Date	Opposition	Goals	Score
Billy Struthers	4 Nov 1882	Bootle	5	6-1
James Cassidy	30 Nov 1889	Derby County	4	7-1
David Weir	18 Jan 1890	Belfast Distillery	4	10-2
James Cassidy	1 Feb 1890	Sheffield United	5	13-0
David Weir	1 Feb 1890	Sheffield United	4	13-0
Charlie Henderson	1 Jan 1895	Derby County	4	6-0
Laurie Bell	28 Apr 1900	Burton Swifts	4	5-0
Albert Shepherd	18 Nov 1905	Nottingham Forest	4	6-0
Albert Shepherd	17 Feb 1906	Sunderland	4	6-2
Joe Smith	3 Jan 1914	Manchester United	4	6-1
Joe Smith	25 Dec 1920	Sunderland	4	6-2
Joe Smith	2 Jan 1923	Nottingham Forest	4	4-2
David Jack	22 Apr 1925	Blackburn Rovers	4	6-0
Harold Blackmore	5 Nov 1927	Burnley	4	7-1
Harold Blackmore	28 Dec 1929	Everton	4	5-0
Jack Milsom	30 Dec 1933	West Ham United	4	5-1
Ray Westwood	6 Oct 1934	Barnsley	4	8-0
Jack Milsom	2 Jan 1935	Burnley	4	7-0
Willie Moir	30 Aug 1948	Aston Villa	4	4-2
Malcolm Barrass	6 Nov 1948	Manchester City	4	5-1
Willie Moir	27 Dec 1948	Sheffield United	4	6-1
Nat Lofthouse	10 Dec 1955	Birmingham City	4	6-0
Tony Caldwell	10 Sep 1983	Walsall	5	8-1

CHAMPIONSHIP IV – 1996/97

In the club's last season at Burnden Park, Colin Todd led the Wanderers to the first division championship in what can only be described as their most enthralling season in the 102 years they had played at the famous ground. Only four teams could lay claim to beating the Whites in a season in which the team set standards and broke records that had been set before the war. One of the highlights was a 7-0 demolition of Swindon Town, with the club just one goal away from equaling their record league score, and doubles over the much-fancied Wolves and Manchester City. After winning at Queens Park Rangers to secure promotion, a 2-1 success at Maine Road four days later secured the championship. There were still five games to play, so the team went all out for the double hundred – 100 goals and 100 points. The 4-1 home win over Charlton Athletic in the final game at Burnden Park set a new record 28th League success. Though the Wanderers drew 2-2 at Tranmere with Jamie Pollock scoring the club's 100th goal of the season, a last-minute equaliser for the Wirral club meant that the Whites had to be satisfied with 98 points.

Football League First Division

	P	W	D	L	F	A	Pts
BOLTON WANDERERS	46	28	14	4	100	53	98
Barnsley	46	22	14	10	76	55	80
Wolverhampton Wanderers	46	22	10	14	68	51	76
Ipswich Town	46	20	14	12	68	50	74
Sheffield United	46	20	13	13	75	52	73
Crystal Palace	46	19	14	13	78	48	71
Portsmouth	46	20	8	18	59	53	68
Port Vale	46	17	16	13	58	55	67
Queens Park Rangers	46	18	12	16	64	60	66
Birmingham City	46	17	15	14	52	48	66
Tranmere Rovers	46	17	14	15	63	56	65
Stoke City	46	18	10	18	51	57	64
Norwich City	46	17	12	21	63	68	63
Manchester City	46	17	10	19	59	60	61
Charlton Athletic	46	16	11	191	52	66	59
West Bromwich Albion	46	14	15	17	68	72	57
Oxford United	46	16	9	21	64	68	57
Reading	46	15	12	19	58	67	57
Swindon Town	46	15	9	22	52	71	54
Huddersfield Town	46	13	15	18	48	61	54
Bradford City	46	12	12	22	47	72	48
Grimsby Town	46	11	13	22	60	81	46
Oldham Athletic	46	10	13	23	51	66	43
Southend United	46	8	15	23	42	86	39

BOLTON'S TOP FA CUP SCORERS

1 Nat Lofthouse...................................... 27
2 Joe Smith 23
3 Billy Struthers.................................... 18
4 James Cassidy 17
4 David Jack.. 17
4 Ray Westwood 17
7 Willie Moir.. 16
8 John Reid Smith 15
9 Harold Blackmore............................... 11
9 Kenny Davenport................................. 11
9 Jack Milsom 11
9 Ray Parry 11

GOALKEEPERS

Bolton have been well served by their goalkeepers and most have been popular with the supporters. The contributions of Eddie Hopkinson and Dick Pym have been highlighted elsewhere in this book. Others of note include Charlie Wright – one of the biggest characters seen at Burnden Park – where he served as player, coach and manager. Among three international appearances for Hong Kong while on National Service in the Lancashire Regiment, he played against Peru and saved a penalty in a 2-1 win. Jim McDonagh has the unusual record of being capped for two different countries: England at youth level and the Republic of Ireland at senior level. Signed from Rotherham United (while playing for the Millers at Burnden Park in November 1972 he presumed the ball had gone out of play, placed it for a goal kick, but Garry Jones nipped in and put the ball into an empty net for the winning goal). While in Bolton colours, he became one of the handful of keepers to score in a league game, netting with a kick downfield in January 1983 as Bolton beat Burnley 3-0. Dave Felgate, a Welsh international who played in over 300 league and cup games, reached 61 Football League appearances without playing once in the competition for Bolton, even though they held his contract! Current keeper, Finnish international Jussi Jaaskelainen, is one of the best in the Premiership and in October 2006 he saved two penalties in the dying moments of a dramatic 1-0 win at Blackburn Rovers.

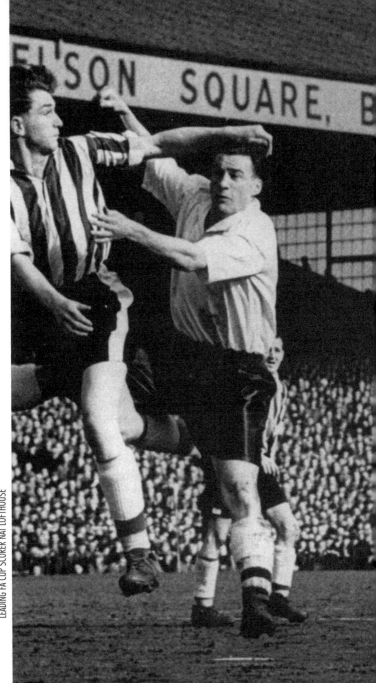

ELSON SQUARE, B

LEADING FA CUP SCORER NAT LOFTHOUSE

TWO CHRISTMAS DAY CRACKERS

If it's goals that make football the magnet then two Christmas Day matches at Burnden Park saw the game at its best. The first in 1920 saw the Wanderers line up against Sunderland without recent acquisition David Jack. He caught a severe cold and though it had been announced that he would make his debut, it would have been unwise to play him. After Jimmy Seddon and Joe Smith had put Bolton 2-0 up courtesy of inch-perfect passes by Jack's replacement Bruce Longworth, Sunderland fought back to level at 2-2 with goals from Buchan and Moore. But then in the last quarter-of-an-hour, Sunderland's defence folded like a pack of cards. It was principally due to Joe Smith, who recorded a hat-trick in the space of five minutes, after the Wearsiders had cast gloom over the crowd by their recovery. Sunderland's new keeper Dempster, signed from a Scottish junior club, would certainly not forget his first visit to Burnden Park as Smith's powerful shots were unstoppable. On scoring his last goal, Smith the hero was so dazed in heading a ball that must have been as heavy as lead, he had to be taken from the field. Frank Roberts rounded off the half-dozen for Bolton who ran out winners 6-2. The 1952 Christmas Day game at Burnden Park saw Arsenal the visitors and they could have been behind in under a minute but Willie Moir dragged his shot wide. Bolton's Scottish international forward made amends moments later to put the Wanderers 1-0 up but on 12 minutes, Arthur Milton dribbled round a couple of defenders to level the scores. Webster shot against an upright and Moir saw his header beat Kelsey but land on the roof of the net. Despite all Bolton's pressure it was Arsenal who went in at half-time 2-1 up after Cliff Holton netted just before the interval. Two goals in the opening five minutes of the second-half through Roper and Logie demonstrated the London club's mastery of the heavy conditions. Bolton didn't buckle and Lofthouse soon reduced the arrears. Arsenal promptly added two more through a Daniel spot-kick and another Holton drive to lead 6-2 but the margin was again reduced courtesy of goals by Lofthouse and Moir. Five minutes from the end, Bobby Langton won a penalty. He took the spot-kick himself but placed his shot too near the keeper who was able to save. Kelsey also made a tremendous save from Nat Lofthouse in the dying moments and Arsenal travelled back to Highbury with both points after their 6-4 win.

QUEEN'S CHRISTMAS DAY SPEECH

During the Queen's Christmas Day speech of 1971, references to Bolton were made by Princes Andrew and Edward. During the programme, the Princes were shown photographs of the Bolton v Manchester City 1926 FA Cup Final and Prince Andrew said: "Bolton Wanderers are now in the second division or third." Bolton chairman John Banks wrote to Buckingham Palace: 'Your sons spoke felicitously of the Bolton Wanderers' team which won the FA Cup in 1926 and made somewhat sympathetic references to the present team. To mark the occasion, the club has presumed to send the two Princes club scarves as gifts in the hope that it will be a reminder of a happy Christmas occasion.'

MR CONSISTENCY

On leaving school, Alex Finney worked down the pits and was a left full-back for South Liverpool before signing for New Brighton. It was whilst playing for New Brighton in the Lancashire Junior cup final at Burnden Park against Chorley that he was spotted by the Wanderers. The Rakers unaccountably forgot to place the defender's name on their retained list and Bolton lost no time in signing him. After making his debut in a 2-0 defeat at Birmingham in September 1922, he soon established himself in the side and formed a good understanding with right-back Bob Haworth. Finney was the mainstay of the Bolton defence that kept the Hammers at bay in the 1923 FA Cup Final when at the age of just 22, he was the youngest member of the side. In 1923-24 he was the club's only ever-present as they finished fourth in the First Division. A cartilage operation cost Finney his place in the 1926 FA Cup winning team but he was back for Bolton's 2-0 win over Portsmouth in 1929. Although he was one of the finest full-backs in the country, full international honours eluded him. However, in 1928, Finney did play for the Football League when they beat the Irish League at St James Park, Newcastle 9-1. He played the last of his 530 first team games for the Wanderers on New Year's Day 1937, the last player on the club's books to have played in the cup finals of the 1920s. He then played for Darwen until the outbreak of the Second World War which, with the suspension of football, ended his career. After hanging up his boots, he moved to Wallasey where he worked for the Local Corporation until his retirement.

REEBOK STADIUM

The new 25,000 all-seater Reebok Stadium, which was constructed to Fifa and Uefa recommendations, provides some of the finest spectator facilities to be found anywhere in Europe – at a cost of £35 million. Adjoining the Reebok Stadium is the Middlebrook Development, where more than 3,000 jobs have been created. The spectators at the Reebok – which now has a capacity of 28,723 – are accommodated in lower and upper tiers and because of the sweeping curves of the upper tier no-one is ever seated more than 90 metres from the centre of the playing area. The stadium has 46 executive box suites and the eight spectator concourses have concession units selling fans a variety of foods, that can be consumed in view of one of the play-back TV screens in operation around the ground. The reception foyer houses two lifts, which take guests up to three floors where corporate executive areas can cater for over 2,000 people on match days. At the end of August 1997, a crowd of over 10,000 spectators turned up for a 'dry run' to look around the stadium for the first time and watch a short game between the club's youngsters. The first visitors to the Reebok were Everton on 1 September 1997. The first goal to be scored in the stadium came from the boot of Alan Thompson as he netted a penalty in a 1-1 draw with Spurs. The FA honoured the stadium by hosting internationals at women's under-17, under-20 and under-21 levels, something that had never been seen at the Wanderers' other homes. The stadium has also hosted international rugby league matches with visits from both Australia and New Zealand as well as the World Club Championship won by St Helens. The Reebok has also hosted concerts featuring such famous acts as Oasis, Elton John and Coldplay whilst the UK Open Darts Championship and boxing matches with local boxer Amir Khan have been held here. Below are the last five season's average league attendances at The Reebok:

2003-04	26,795
2004-05	26,006
2005-06	26,265
2006-07	23,282
2007-08	20,901

NON-LEAGUE OPPONENTS

The Wanderers have encountered 36 non-League opponents in FA Cup ties, the last being in January 2001 when they narrowly defeated Yeovil Town 2-1. Linfield Athletic of Belfast were the first non-League club to put Bolton out of the FA Cup in November 1888. Bolton did have some excuse for going down 4-0. They had to send their reserve side to play the tie in Ireland as the first team were involved in a Football League game against West Bromwich Albion on the same day. In February 1890, the Wanderers recorded their best score in any of the major competitions with a 13-0 win over then non-League Sheffield United at Pikes Lane. The club reached the semi-finals that season only to go down 2-1 to Sheffield Wednesday, who were then members of the Football Alliance, at Perry Barr, Birmingham. One of the club's greatest upsets occurred in February 1901, when the Wanderers riding high in the first division faced Southern League Reading. The Biscuitmen had been at Nettlebed, one of the highest points in the South of England and had spent the night at Bolton's historical Swan Hotel in the town centre. Reading took the lead through Sharp who shot past the advancing Sutcliffe and though Bolton maintained a terrific assault on the Reading goal, they hung on to record a 1-0 victory – Burnden Park had seen its first FA Cup shock! Bolton have been knocked out of the FA Cup by non-League opposition on six occasions, the last being in January 1911 when Midland League side Chesterfield won 2-0 at Burnden. The Wanderers were top of the Second Division at the time but went down to two goals by part-timer Revill, who was a coal miner. In January 1914, Bolton entertained Swindon Town who were then leaders of the Southern League. The Wiltshire club had caused an upset by beating Manchester United in the previous round. The crowd that day was 50,558 – the best for a game against non-League opposition and they witnessed a Joe Smith hat-trick in a 4-2 win for the Wanderers. Since the war, the Wanderers have been drawn against non-League opposition on ten occasions and have been able to qualify for the next round at the first time of asking with one exception. In January 1964, the Wanderers needed a Francis Lee penalty to earn a replay against Bath City but ran out comfortable 3-0 winners in the replay at Burnden Park.

ALL AROUND THE WORLD

There was a time when most of Bolton's first team hailed from Farnworth or Westhoughton – with few players coming from anywhere other than the north-west of England. However, things have changed in world football and the players who appeared for Wanderers during the 2007/08 season hailed from around the globe. Including England there were no fewer than 16 different nationalities within the squad, giving a real international feel to the Bolton squad.

Player	Born
Jussi Jaaskelainen	Vaasa, Finland
Ali Ab Habsi	Muscat, Oman
Ian Walker	Watford
Nicky Hunt	Westhoughton
Ricardo Gardner	St Andrew, Jamaica
JLloyd Samuel	Trinidad
Andy O'Brien	Harrogate
Gary Cahill	Sheffield
Gretar Steinsson	Siglufjorour, Iceland
Abdoulaye Meite	Paris, France
Joey O'Brien	Dublin
Mikel Alonso	Tolosa, Spain
Kevin Nolan	Liverpool
Ivan Campo	San Sebastian, Spain
Gavin McCann	Blackpool
Danny Guthrie	Shrewsbury
Stelios Giannakopoulos	Athens, Greece
Matthew Taylor	Oxford
Adranik Teymourian	Tehran, Iran
Daniel Braaten	Oslo, Norway
Kevin Davies	Sheffield
El Hadji Diouf	Dakar, Senegal
Nicolas Anelka	Versailles, France
Ricardo Vaz Te	Lisbon, Portugal
Heldar Helguson	Akureyri, Iceland
Grzegorz Rasiak	Szczecin, Poland

ONE-MATCH WONDERS

At the end of the 2006/07 season these 59 players had appeared in just one Football League match for Bolton Wanderers.

Name	Opponents	Venue	Date
Edward Siddons	West Bromwich Albion...	(a)	5.11.1888
Harry McGuinness	Wolverhampton Wanderers	(a)	10.11.1888
David Mercer	Wolverhampton Wanderers	(a)	10.11.1888
Frederick Dyer	Preston North End	(h)	24.11.1888
James Pearson	West Bromwich Albion	(a)	4.11.1889
John Chirnside	Derby County	(h)	1.1.1892
Arthur Lever	West Bromwich Albion	(h)	7.4.1894
Jack Bracelin	Wolverhampton Wanderers	(a)	27.10.1894
Albert Guest	Blackburn Rovers	(h)	1.11.1894
Edward Hamilton	Preston North End	(h)	14.3.1896
Arthur Hiles	Wolverhampton Wanderers	(a)	20.4.1897
John Low	Stoke City	(a)	12.11.1900
Robert Haslam	Everton	(h)	15.12.1900
William Hodgkiss	Everton	(h)	15.12.1900
George Smith	Aston Villa	(a)	26.12.1900
Peter McWilliams	Sheffield Wednesday	(a)	3.1.1903
Fred Warburton	Leicester Fosse	(h)	3.10.1903
Harry Abbot	Doncaster Rovers	(h)	22.10.1904
Charles Beckett	Middlesbrough	(a)	9.12.1905
Harry King	Woolwich Arsenal	(h)	1.1.1906
William Evans	Nottingham Forest	(a)	15.2.1908
Herbert Tierney	Nottingham Forest	(a)	15.2.1908
Thomas Rollinson	Blackburn Rovers	(a)	29.2.1908
Harry Wilkinson	Nottingham Forest	(a)	16.10.1909
John Pulman	Blackburn Rovers	(a)	26.3.1910
Charlie Hateley	Manchester City	(a)	21.3.1914
John Pickup	West Bromwich Albion	(a)	11.10.1919
John Howarth	West Bromwich Albion	(h)	18.10.1919
Alf Winterburn	West Bromwich Albion	(h)	18.10.1919
Albert Moss	Huddersfield Town	(h)	11.12.1920
John Long	Huddersfield Town	(h)	24.9.1921
Joe Keetley	Manchester United	(h)	8.4.1922

John Johnston ....Sunderland (a) 16.9.1922
James Bryan ....Middlesbrough (h) 18.9.1929
Fred Gorringe ....Leeds United (a)..................................6.12.1930
Eddie Jones ....Lincoln City (a)....................................5.5.1934
Gerry Kirkman ....Brentford (a).......................................28.12.1935
Walter Sidebottom ..Huddersfield Town (h).......................25.2.1939
John Simm ....Wolverhampton Wanderers (a)..........24.4.1948
Dennis Bailey...........Preston North End (a) 20.10.1956
Albert Goulden........Manchester City (a) 13.4.1963
Mike McBurney ......Notts County (h)...............................17.11.1973
Andy Clements........Burnley (a) 20.8.1977
Craig Moores...........Grimsby Town (h)..............................22.11.1980
Paul Booth ....Swansea City (h) 16.2.1985
Neil Matthews.........Notts County (a) 28.3.1987
Ian Callaghan...........Colchester United (a) 11.12.1987
Andy Kennedy.........Chester City (a)..................................26.10.1991
Gerry Peyton............Exeter City (h).....................................22.2.1992
Jamie Fullarton ....Oxford United (a)..................................3.4.1999
Akin Bulent ....Aston Villa (a) 1.1.2003
Delroy Facey ....Manchester United (a) 16.8.2003
John Otsemobor ......Manchester City (h)...........................21.2.2004
Blessing Kaku ....West Bromwich Albion (a) 2.10.2004
Andy Oakes ....Aston Villa (h)...................................13.11.2004
Fabrice Fernandes ....Chelsea (a) 15.10.2005
Jaroslaw Fojut...........Portsmouth (a).......................................1.2.2006
Johann Smith...........Manchester United (h).....................28.10.2006
Cesar Martin............Chelsea (a) 28.4.2007

NO OFFSIDE!

On 28 March 1925, Bolton Wanderers took on Manchester City in a friendly at Burnden Park. There was nothing unusual in that, except for the fact that both sides were taking part in a new offside rule proposal. A crowd of just 4,621 turned up to see the game played with no offisdes awarded within 40 yards from goal. Bolton won the game 3-0 with goals from Idwal Davies, David Jack and Joe Smith, all of which came in the space of ten minutes midway through the first half.

UEFA CUP 2007-08

Bolton began their group games with a home game against Portuguese side Braga. Nicolas Anelka wasted a glorious first half chance before substitute El-Hadji Diouf nodded Bolton ahead from a Kevin Davies cross after the break. But, with new boss Gary Megson looking on from the dug-out before he officially took over the following day, Bolton began to struggle and Braga substitute Jailson leveled the scores with a fine looping header to deny the Whites a morale-boosting victory. With the club languishing at second-from-bottom of the Premiership, Megson took his side to Bayern Munich for their second group game. The Germans were unbeaten in all competitions and sitting pretty at the top of the Bundesliga. But the Wanderers made a dream start when Ricardo Gardner bundled in a deflected shot off the crossbar after Kevin Nolan's long throw caused chaos in the box. Lukas Podolski equalised for the home side on the half-hour before claiming his second just after the break. But then on 82 minutes, Kevin Davies grabbed an unlikely draw for the Wanderers when he slipped the ball under keeper Oliver Kahn. His strike sealed an epic European result for struggling Bolton. In the home game against Greek side Aris Salonika, Bolton struggled to find any momentum and fell behind to a Calvo goal on the stroke of half-time. But Bolton's own Greek, Stelios, probably the best player on the field on the night, struck in stoppage time to salvage a point, poking home Mikel Alonso's cross. The Wanderers' final group match saw them travel to Belgrade where they faced Red Star. The Whites moved to the brink of qualification from the group stages after Gavin McCann scored the only goal of the game. After going through the group stages unbeaten, Bolton went temporarily top of the group table as all the other sides had a game to play. All they could do now was to sit and wait.

Final Group Table

	P	W	D	L	F	A	Pts
Bayern Munich	4	2	2	0	12	5	8
Braga	4	1	3	0	5	3	6
BOLTON WANDERERS	4	1	3	0	5	4	6
Aris Salonika	4	1	2	1	5	8	5
Red Star Belgrade	4	0	0	4	2	9	0

In the last 32 of the Uefa Cup, Bolton drew one of the fancied sides Atletico Madrid, a side at the time fourth in La Liga. The Whites had keeper Jussi Jaaskelainen to thank for keeping the scores level with a world-class one-handed save to deny Atletico's Antonio Lopez. But the complexion of the match shifted in Bolton's favour when Madrid substitute Aguero was sent off for spitting after 74 minutes; it was only a matter of moments later that El-Hadji Diouf fired what proved to be the winner from six yards out. The victory gave Megson's side an enormous psychological fillip for the return leg. Despite Bolton's first-leg advantage, the odds were still stacked against the Whites as they lined up at the Vicente Calderon stadium. The Wanderers more than held their own with a battling display, frustrating the home side, who had never lost at home to an English club in European competition. With the game ending in a goalless draw, Bolton had claimed another famous scalp to reach the last 16 of the competition. Sadly, though, the evening was spoilt by what the Wanderers described as "overzealous and disproportionate treatment" of the club's fans by Spanish police and they lodged an official complaint with Uefa. Bolton's next opponents were Sporting Lisbon and though Kevin Nolan was out with a back injury and El-Hadji Diouf was suspended, Bolton, who lost Jussi Jaaskelainen in the warm-up to injury, went ahead after 25 minutes through Gavin McCann. The midfielder's strike, though, was cancelled out after Simon Vukcevic cracked a stunning strike past Ali Al Habsi. The game then could have gone either way but it ended 1-1 and though the club were still unbeaten in the Uefa Cup competition this season, they knew they would have to conjure another of their away-day specials if the European adventure was to continue. Manager Gary Megson's priority was clearly survival in the Premiership as he left seven available regular first-team players in England. After the 1-1 draw at home in the first leg, a goal for Bolton was a necessity but the makeshift side struggled to make many chances. Ricardo Vaz Te had the Wanderers' best chance but he drove his shot into the side-netting. The club tried to adopt a more adventurous approach with their exit looming but left themselves exposed as the game wore on and Sporting eventually took advantage when Bruno Pererinha curled in a shot.

GINGER MOURINHO

Nicknamed 'Ginger Mourinho' Bolton manager Gary Megson replaced out-going boss Sammy Lee at The Reebok in October 2007 on a two-and-a-half year deal. He left Leicester City – then in the Championship – after just a month in charge at the Walkers Stadium, and accepting he was the not the number one choice (Bolton already had approaches for Steve Bruce and Chris Coleman rejected) Megson inherited a tough challenge with the club very much embroiled in the Premiership relegation dogfight – but Megson was up for the challenge. As a player, he was a tough-tackling defensive midfielder and something of a journeyman, playing for nine different clubs. Born in Manchester he started his professional career in the south-west with Plymouth Argyle, from whom he left to join Everton – but after failing to establish himself at Goodison Park, moved to his father Don's old stomping ground, Sheffield Wednesday (his dad played over 350 games for Wednesday, during a ten-year spell from 1959-69). Megson junior played in an FA Cup semi-final in 1983 and was a member of their team that gained promotion to the top flight in 1983-84 but, in 1984, after three years at Hillsborough he was signed by Nottingham Forest. Sold by Brian Clough to Newcastle United without making a first team appearance, he rejoined the Owls in 1985. Transferred to Manchester City, he played three seasons at Maine Road before joining Norwich City, helping the Canaries reach the UEFA Cup after finishing third in the Premiership. He later finished his playing career with spells at Lincoln City and Shrewsbury Town. At Norwich he had had a brief spell as caretaker-manager but his first full managerial post was at Blackpool in 1996. He then managed Stockport County and Stoke City before taking over the reigns at West Bromwich Albion where he twice took the Baggies into the Premiership. Spells at Nottingham Forest and Leicester City followed before he arrived at The Reebok. He recorded his first win, 1-0 over eventual champions Manchester United and took the club into the last 16 of the UEFA Cup for the first time in their history. He also secured his first survival as a Premiership manager when the club remained unbeaten for their last five games of the campaign.

GARY MEGSON EMBRACES IAN NOLAN AFTER WANDERERS SECURE THEIR PREMIERSHIP STATUS IN 2008

ASSORTED LEAGUE RECORDS

Consecutive Wins .... 11 in 1904/05
Consecutive Defeats .... 11 in 1901/02, 1902/03
Consecutive Games Unbeaten................................... 23 in 1990/91
Consecutive Games Without a Win .... 26 in 1901/02, 1902/03
Most Points in a Season .... 98 (3 points) in 1996/97
.... 61 (2 points) in 1972/73
Fewest Points in a Season......................... 29 (3 points) in 1995/96
.... 19 (2 points) in 1889/90 and 1902/03
Most Goals Scored.. 100 in 1996/97
Fewest Goals Scored... 28 in 1897/98
Most Goals Conceded.. 92 in 1932/33
Fewest Goals Conceded .... 25 in 1899/1900

THE NUTTALL FAMILY

Jack Nuttall had become Bolton's first trainer groundsman at Pikes
Lane in 1887. It was most definitely a family affair as the team's
laundry was his wife's responsibility. When the club moved to
Burnden Park in 1895, the Nuttalls moved to a house adjacent to
the club's new ground with Jack looking after both responsibilities
until 1903 when former Wolves and Everton player Jack Lewis
took over training duties. Nuttall continued to act as the club's
groundsman. Two years after the Nuttall's had moved, their son
Harry was born and he was to follow in the footsteps of elder
brother Jimmy in playing for the Wanderers. Jimmy Nuttall had
played in 82 games for the Whites during the First World War
whilst Harry began his career with Fleetwood. He returned to
Bolton in 1921 and after signing for the Wanderers, made his
debut in a 1-0 home win over FA Cup holders Tottenham Hotspur.
After settling into the half-back position, he made 326 first team
appearances and won three FA Cup medals and made three full
international appearances for England. He left the Wanderers in
1932 to join Rochdale and later coached Nelson before returning
'home' to Burnden Park in 1935. He was the club's reserve team
trainer until his retirement in 1964, later taking on the duties of kit
man until his death in 1969.

BIONIC SAM!

On 27 December 1975, 42,680 turned up for Bolton's top-of-the-table clash with Sunderland. It was the biggest crowd at Burnden Park since Manchester United's visit 13 years earlier. As kick-off time approached, there were still hundreds of fans trying to get inside the ground to watch a game that proved to be of the highest quality. The opening half definitely belonged to the Black Cats, the Second Division leaders and they could have been three goals to the good but for the heroics of Barry Siddall. As it was, they went in at half-time 1-0 up thanks to a scrappy goal when Wanderers' full-back Tony Dunne barged into a Tony Towers free-kick to send the ball past the Bolton keeper. Sunderland then began to sit on their lead and Bolton drew level with one of Burnden Park's most classic goals. Sam Allardyce rose majestically between Jack Ashurst and Joe Bolton to power the ball with his forehead past Jim Montgomery. The ground erupted to salute what was a magnificent goal. The Wanderers won the game when John Byrom headed home Peter Thompson's cross to send the Whites level at the top of the table with the then Roker Park club.

LAST DAY AT THE BRIDGE

The Wanderers have had vital last day games against Chelsea at Stamford Bridge in recent years with very differing outcomes. On the final day of the 1997-98 season, Chelsea beat Bolton 2-0 to condemn the Trotters to relegation from the Premiership. The home crowd, though, would have preferred to have seen Everton relegated and chanted 'let 'em score' as the Wanderers mounted a series of desperate attacks in the closing minutes. Sadly for the Trotters the Blues' defence ignored the chants. On 11 May 2008, Bolton were again scheduled to play their final game of the campaign at Stamford Bridge. This time, only a mathematical phenomenon would send the Whites down but Chelsea began the day still hoping to win the Premiership title. Even after Shevchenko gave Chelsea the lead, they failed to build on this and with rivals Manchester United winning at Wigan, Matt Taylor struck in injury-time to earn the Wanderers an impressive draw.